ESL VIDEO LIBF

FOCUS ON AMERICAN CULTURE

ELIZABETH HENLY

REGENTS/PRENTICE HALL

Acquisitions Editor: **Nancy L. Leonhardt**
Development Editor: **Stephanie Karras**
Editorial Assistance: **D. Andrew Gitzy, Terry TenBarge**
Prepress Buyer: **Ray Keating**
Manufacturing Buyer: **Lori Bulwin**
Cover Supervisor: **Marianne Frasco**
Cover Design: **Ruta Kysilewskyj**
Cover Photograph: **© 1992 Arthur Tilley/FPG International**
Interior Design: **Tom Nery**
Technical Support: **Molly Pike Riccardi, Freddy Flake**

ISBN 0-13-007113-7

TABLE OF CONTENTS

ACKNOWLEDGMENTS

I am indebted to various people who have made this book possible and would like to thank them for their valuable contributions.

First and foremost I would like to express my heartfelt appreciation to Donna Brinton of the University of California at Los Angeles, whom I consider a mentor as well as a friend. Her guidance and encouragement in addition to the substantive contributions she made to this project have been invaluable.

This book may have never made it through the final stages without the editorial guidance of Susan Stempleski. I have learned much about materials development and the editing process from her and am grateful for her expert assistance and suggestions.

Many people at Regents/Prentice Hall have worked tirelessly on this project. I would like to thank Nancy Leonhardt for the opportunity to write this book. I thank Stephanie Karras especially for the endless hours and care she took to do what had to be done to meet seemingly impossible deadlines. There are many others on the editorial and production staff at Regents/Prentice Hall to whom I owe gratitude for their work on this book as well.

My family and husband have supported me throughout. I thank Tom for putting up with me and assisting me emotionally when I needed it the most.

Finally, this book is dedicated to my brother, John, for his courage.

INTRODUCTION

The *ABC News* ESL Video Library is a series of interactive, task-based integrated skills texts for adult learners of English as a second or foreign language. Each text is accompanied by a video, which contains the core presentation of language, and an instructor's manual, which includes an answer key as well as complete transcripts of all the video segments. This video series is unique in that it uses actual broadcast footage from internationally known *ABC News* programs such as *Business World, PrimeTime Live, 20/20, Nightline, The Health Show,* and *World News Tonight* to stimulate students' interest in timely topics presented by world-famous anchors and reporters. More important, these broadcast segments provide authentic language input in real situations — nothing has been staged or "set up" artificially. Instead, language instruction flows from the natural language used and is thus always presented and practiced in context.

Each of the texts (*Focus on Business, Focus on Innovators and Innovations, Focus on the Environment, Focus on Health,* and *Focus on American Culture*) presents lively topics that are of interest to international students and that relate to life in the United States and abroad. Students are encouraged to see U.S. culture in the context of the global village and to bring in their own cultural views to analyze and interpret the video segments.

The instruction utilizes an interactive approach, providing many opportunities for students to work in pairs, small groups, and teams. Students are encouraged to pool their knowledge and learn from one another. The teacher functions as a facilitator, guiding students through tasks that enable them to discover and learn on their own.

To make the videos easy to use, time codes have been included in the upper right-hand corner of the screen. These time codes are cross-referenced in the texts so that you can easily find your place on the video. This feature also makes it easier to replay sections you find particularly useful or difficult as many times as you want.

The materials for each segment are divided into five sections: Previewing, Global Viewing, Intensive Viewing, Language Focus, and Postviewing. The purpose of each section is as follows:

Previewing challenges students to predict what the segment will cover. This section also helps activate the students' schema and enables the teacher to know what background information students bring to class. This section also presents essential vocabulary that the students will need to know in order to understand the segment.

Global Viewing develops students' understanding of the key ideas presented in the segment. In this section, students' overall comprehension and ability to look for main ideas are stressed.

Intensive Viewing zeroes in on specific items for comprehension to prepare students for the Postviewing tasks. Students practice looking and listening for details in activities such as notetaking and cloze-type exercises.

Language Focus gives practice in vocabulary and expressions students will need to use to complete the Postviewing tasks. Occasionally, an interesting point of language structure from the video segment is reviewed and practiced.

Postviewing provides a wealth of additional materials, such as readings, graphs, and questionnaires, all related to the topic of the segment. The final tasks pull together all the language and content skills the students have practiced in the segment.

An additional feature of the videos is that all of the programs, with the exception of *Business World*, are closed-captioned. If you have access to a decoder (or if your television has the new decoder chip), you can open up the captions and see the written transcriptions of what the speakers are saying as they speak.

FOCUS ON AMERICAN CULTURE

Focus on American Culture looks at four aspects of the lifestyle in the United States: family, work, education, and trends. By careful viewing and discussion of the news reports on each of these topics, students will increase their understanding of the culture and cultural diversity found in the United States. As students focus on the content of the video segments, specific language skills will be practiced.

In the **Previewing**, **Global Viewing**, **Intensive Viewing**, and **Language Focus** sections, the content of the video is used as a springboard for a variety of activities — including predicting, understanding the main idea, and notetaking — and for exercises focusing on specific vocabulary and expressions used by the speakers in the video.

The **Postviewing** section includes a variety of tasks that expand on the topic introduced in the video. The Comparing Cultures exercise in this section helps the student gain insight into American culture through provocative questions that lead to class discussions. In addition, students make comparisons between the culture of his or her own country and that of the United States. Also in this section the vocabulary and language structures and functions presented earlier in the segment are integrated into the postviewing tasks. Activities such as readings, discussions, debates, role plays, surveys, and writing assignments allow students to react to ideas presented in the video segments and give their own opinions about what they have viewed. Following is a summary of the language functions in the postviewing tasks at the end of each segment of the text.

Unit 1: The Family in America

Segment & Topic	Functions in Postviewing Tasks
1 Mid-life Moms	• Comparing cultural trends in motherhood • Reading about U.S. family trends and comparing them to other cultures • Conducting a survey about family trends • Writing up the results of the survey

Unit 1:The Family in America (continued)

Segment & Topic	Functions in Postviewing Tasks
2 Fast-Track Parents	• Comparing cultural trends in parenting • Reading about and researching baby boomer lifestyle trends • Comparing generational differences in lifestyles • Writing an essay • Role playing
3 Is Love Color-blind?	• Comparing cultural views on transracial adoption • Determining the bias of a reading • Using evidence to support an opinion • Debating the issue of transracial adoption • Writing an opinion essay

Unit 2: Work in America

Segment & Topic	Functions in Postviewing Tasks
4 Manufacturers Engage in False Advertising on the Environment	• Comparing cultural differences in business concerns about the environment • Reading about and discussing "green consumerism" • Investigating the environmental concerns of business • Reporting and writing up the investigation • Writing a letter to the editor of the local newspaper • Comparing cultural differences in opinions of the impact of technology • Reading about and discussing advances in communication • Planning and presenting products for the future • Writing about the future

Unit 2: Work in America (continued)

Segment & Topic	Functions in Postviewing Tasks
6 The Joys and Risks of the "Daddy Track"	• Comparing cultural differences concerning men's contribution to childcare • Reading about the emergence of the "daddy track" • Expressing your opinion about companies and their concerns about families • Discussing the implications of the Family-Leave Bill • Conducting a survey about career versus family attitudes • Presenting a skit about the "daddy track" • Writing up the results of a survey • Writing a reaction paper

Unit 3: Education in America

Segment & Topic	Functions in Postviewing Tasks
7 Bilingual Education	• Comparing cultural differences in opinions of language and education • Reading and discussing the idea of an official language • Debating the issue of bilingual education • Writing an opinion essay
8 Judgement Day	• Comparing cultural differences in higher education systems • Arguing for or against your opinion • Supporting your argument • Writing a college application essay

Unit 3: Education in America (continued)

Segment & Topic	Functions in Postviewing Tasks
9 Cheating in College	• Comparing cultural attitudes about cheating in college • Reading about solutions to cheating • Brainstorming solutions to cheating • Serving on a task force and presenting your proposal • Writing about and supporting an opinion

Unit 4: Trends in America

Segment & Topic	Functions in Postviewing Tasks
10 New Suburban Designs for Living	• Comparing cultural views about suburban living • Reading about alternatives to the suburbs • Planning an ideal community • Presenting a plan of an ideal community • Writing an opinion
11 Health Care for the Poor	• Comparing cultural differences in health care systems • Reading about solutions to the health care crisis • Inferring bias from contextual clues • Taking part in a round table discussion
12 The Perfect Baby: A Follow-Up	• Comparing the issue of genetic engineering across cultures • Reading about and discussing genetic engineering • Planning for future uses of genetic engineering • Researching issues in medical ethics • Writing a marketing plan

Suggestions for Self-Study

Although best used in a classroom setting with a teacher facilitating your progress, *Focus on American Culture*, can be used for self-study as well. Following are some suggestions that will help you use this textbook and video on your own.

• The exercises in the Previewing, Global Viewing and Intensive Viewing sections are designed to be used in conjunction with the viewing of each video segment. If used according to the directions, these exercises will help you increase your understanding of the content of each video segment.

• The exercises in the Language Focus sections are closely related to language structures contained in the video segments. After working through the Language Focus exercises, you may want to watch and listen to the video again to reinforce your knowledge of these structures you have just practiced by hearing them used in their authentic context.

• While it will be more difficult for you to complete many of the interactive exercises in the Postviewing section, it would be helpful for you to think over your answers to the questions posed in the Comparing Cultures exercises. If possible, find someone who knows the U.S. very well or, better yet, is a native of the U.S. with whom you can discuss your answers. In doing so, you will gain insight into the cultural issues highlighted in each segment.

• The Instructor's Manual will provide you with answers to those questions which have a clear-cut answer. Check the Manual after completing each exercise to see how you are doing. For those exercises which ask for an opinion or are interactive in nature, an answer will not be given in the Instructor's Manual. You may want to find a person to work with so that you can compare answers to such exercises.

• After working through all the exercises in a segment, you may want to watch the entire video segment one more time to see how much your comprehension of it has improved.

• Another useful option for those students who are working alone is to make use of the closed captions. If you have a decoder, you can follow along with the speaker and read the words on the screen. If you do not have a decoder, you can use the transcripts in the Instructor's Manual to reinforce and test your understanding of the videos.

Segment 1

Mid-life Moms

> from *20/20*, 9/6/90
> Runtime: 15:03
> Begin: 00:00:55

Previewing

KEY QUESTIONS

1. Why are some American women postponing having children until they reach mid-life?
2. What are some risks associated with having a baby later in life?
3. What medical tests have played a role in the trend among American women to have children at a later age?
4. What is the ideal, or optimal, age for a woman to have a baby?

DISCUSSION

1. How old was your mother when you were born?

_____

_____

2. What do you think is the best age to start having children? Why?

_____

_____

3. If there is a big difference between the age your mother had her first child and the age you plan to have your first child, why do you think this difference exists?

_____

_____

PREDICTION

Based on the title of this segment, *Mid-life Moms*, the discussion you've had with your classmates, and your own knowledge, what information do you think will be included in this video segment?

1. _____

2. _____

3. _____

4. _____

Note: After you have watched the entire segment once, come back to this section and confirm your predictions by circling any that were correct.

ESSENTIAL WORDS TO KNOW

The following words are used in this video segment. Fill in the blank with the word below that best completes the sentence.

obstetrician	miscarriage	menopause
biological time clocks	chromosome	conceive

1. While most women used to _____ their first child while they were in their 20s, many women today wait until they are much older.

2. As childless women reach a certain age, they sometimes feel their _____ ticking and decide the time to have a child is now.

3. One of the risks of having a child after the age of 35 is the higher possibility that the child will be born with an extra _____, which results in a genetic problem called Down's syndrome.

4. Another risk of late childbirth is a high rate of _____.

5. Because of the increased dangers for older mothers and their babies, it is important that a woman in her 30s see an _____ as soon as she knows she is pregnant.

6. After a woman reaches a certain age in mid-life, she experiences _____ and can no longer get pregnant.

Global Viewing

GETTING THE GENERAL IDEA

00:00:55-
00:15:47

First read the statements below. Then watch the entire video segment and decide whether each statement is true or false. Write *T* or *F*.

_____ 1. In the U.S. the number of women who had their first child after the age of 40 decreased significantly in the 1980s.

_____ 2. The women in this video had successful careers before they had their first children.

_____ 3. Women who have their first child over the age of 40 have no more medical problems than younger women do.

_____ 4. New technological tests have made it possible to determine whether the child a pregnant woman carries has certain genetic problems.

_____ 5. The mid-life moms in this video would encourage older women to have a child.

_____ 6. The ideal age for a woman to have a child is when she is in her early 20s.

Intensive Viewing

GETTING THE FACTS

00:00:50-
00:11:33

Read over the questions below. Then watch this part of the segment again and circle the best response.

1. In what age group are the first-time mothers Dr. Timothy Johnson interviews?
   a. Their 30s.
   b. Their 40s.
   c. Their 20s.
   d. Their teens.

2. According to the Census Bureau, how has the number of women who have had their first child over the age of 40 changed during the 1980s?
   a. It has increased by three times the previous number.
   b. It has decreased by three times the previous number.
   c. It has increased by twice the previous number.
   d. It has increased by four times the previous number.

3. What did Susan and Cathie do before they became mid-life moms?
   a. Cathie had a career, and Susan was a housewife.
   b. Cathie was a housewife, and Susan had a career.
   c. They both had good careers.
   d. They were both housewives.

4. Approximately what percentage of women over the age of 40 are able to conceive?
   a. 70 percent.
   b. 60 percent.
   c. 50 percent.
   d. 40 percent.

5. How does the rate of miscarriage differ between women in their 30s and women in their 40s?
   a. Women in their 40s are half as likely to have a miscarriage as those in their 30s.
   b. Women in their 30s are half as likely to have a miscarriage as those in their 40s.
   c. Women in their 40s are three times as likely to have a miscarriage as those in their 30s.
   d. None of the above.

6. Why are the tests amniocentesis and chorionic villae sampling given?
   a. To determine if a women might have a miscarriage.
   b. To determine whether the mother has a kind of diabetes.
   c. To figure out how large the fetus is.
   d. To determine if the fetus has certain chromosomal problems.

7. What other risks do pregnant women over 40 have?
   a. High blood pressure.
   b. A kind of diabetes.
   c. Having a child with Down's syndrome.
   d. All of the above.

8. During her pregnancy Susan developed which of the following?
   a. High blood pressure.
   b. A kind of diabetes.
   c. Genetic abnormalities.
   d. All of the above.

9. What happened during the birth of Susan's baby?
   a. Susan experienced a lot of pain.
   b. The baby didn't drop into the birth canal.
   c. Susan had a Caesarean section.
   d. All of the above.

10. How big was Suzanna, Susan's baby, at birth?
    a. Six pounds and five ounces.
    b. Six and a half pounds.
    c. Seven pounds and one ounce.
    d. Seven and a half pounds.

TRUE OR FALSE?

First read the statements below. Then watch this part of the segment and decide whether the statement is true or false. Write *T* or *F*.

00:11:52-
00:15:15

_____ 1. Medical problems are not the only kind of problems older parents will face.

_____ 2. Susan feels she will be able to act just like a 20-year-old mother.

_____ 3. Cathie is so tired out from caring for her child that she goes to bed at nine-thirty every night.

_____ 4. Many older mothers who have established their careers have the privilege of hiring someone to help care for their child.

_____ 5. Psychological problems, such as already being in her mid-sixties when her daughter is 21, are very troubling for Cathie.

_____ 6. Biologically, the ideal age to have a child is when a woman is in her late 20s.

Language Focus

AGE EXPRESSIONS: LISTENING CLOZE EXERCISE

Read the sentences below. Then watch the video and fill in the blanks with the missing age expressions.

Downs: How old was your mother when you were born? If you're

_____ , she probably was

_____ ,or maybe even in her teens.

00:00:55-
00:01:03

Downs: In recent years, more women like those you're about to meet are holding off motherhood until at least their _____.

00:01:25-
00:01:32

Dr. Johnson: Cathie Cook gave birth to Abigail, also her first child,

_____.

00:02:20-
00:02:28

Dr. Johnson: Cathie is not alone. She's one of a growing number of women _____ starting families and breaking the so-called biological time clock barrier. According to the Census Bureau, the number of women who had their first child _____ tripled

00:02:50-
00:03:30

during the 1980s. However, this trend does raise some questions. For example, how great is the medical risk for the mother or the child? And is it fair psychologically to have a child born to a woman who is already in _____? These are important questions, but for many women _____ and 40s who worry about their biological time clock, this trend is clearly good news.

COMPREHENSION CHECK

Look over the age expressions you wrote down in the Listening Cloze exercise and answer the following questions.

1. Which phrase describes an exact age? _____

2. Which phrase describes the age of people between the ages of 36 and 40? _____

3. Which two phrases mean "older than 40"? _____

4. Which phrase means "an age between 40 and 44"? _____

5. What word can be added after age 20, 30, etc., to show that the age is older than this? _____

PRACTICE USING AGE EXPRESSIONS

Use some of the age expressions you learned. Ask a partner questions about how old your partner was or thinks he or she will be when he or she _____.

graduates from college   gets a job
gets married   retires
has a child   becomes a grandparent

WORD FORMS

Fill in the blank with the correct form of the words given for each pair of sentences.

1. pregnancy (noun)   pregnant (adjective)
    a. Three months after they were married, Susan found out she was

    _____ .

    b. In Cathie's case, her _____ was not problematic.

2. conception (noun)   conceive (verb)
    a. When it comes to _____, only one-half of all women over the age of 40 can get pregnant.
    b. Once a woman over the age of 40 _____ , she is almost twice as likely to have a miscarriage as a woman in her 30s.

3. genes (noun) genetic (adjective)
   a. Tests like amniocentesis and chorionic villae sampling can detect certain _____ abnormalities in the fetus.
   b. The _____ of the parents pass on physical traits such as eye color, hair color, and height to their unborn child.

4. parents (noun) parental (adjective)
   a. Will some children have to take on an unfair responsibility because of their aging _____?
   b. Some of the financial problems that younger parents face may not be as serious a problem as other _____ responsibilities for older mothers and fathers.

5. energy (noun) energetic (adjective)
   a. At the age of 46, Cathie may not be as _____ as a mother in her 20s.
   b. Even though she may not have as much _____ as a 20-year-old, Cathie feels that she can bring some experience and wisdom into her daughter's life.

Postviewing

COMPARING CULTURES

Discuss the following questions in small groups.

1. Were you surprised or shocked by anything you learned from this video?

2. Do you think the trend toward postponing motherhood until later in life will have positive, negative, or both positive and negative effects on the family?

3. Why do you think this trend is now occurring in the United States?

4. Both Susan and Cathie shared certain similarities in their lifestyles; for example, they were both successful career women who had delayed marriage. Do you think the trend to postpone having children is common among women of all lifestyles in the United States?

5. Is such a trend occurring in your country? Why or why not?

RELATED READING: A TECHNOLOGICAL BREAKTHROUGH

Read the article *At 52, Woman Is Oldest in U.S. to Have In-Vitro Baby* and answer the comprehension and opinion questions that follow.

At 52, Woman Is Oldest in U.S. to Have In-Vitro Baby
by Sherry Joe

A 52-year-old mother was expected to return home today after apparently making history by becoming the oldest woman in the United States to give birth to an in-vitro–fertilized baby.

Jonie Mosby Mitchell of Ventura delivered robust 7-pound, 19-inch Morgan Bradford Mitchell about 4 p.m. Tuesday at Good Samaritan Hospital in Los Angeles.

In vitro is a process by which an egg and sperm are joined in a laboratory and incubated. The resulting embryo is implanted in a woman's uterus.

"As far as we know, she is the oldest woman in the United States to have [a baby after] in-vitro fertilization and the third oldest in the world," said Sara Kaufman, hospital spokeswoman. A 54-year-old Italian woman is the oldest, Kaufman said.

Mitchell, who has already entered menopause, received a donor egg from a 30-year-old woman and the egg was fertilized by Mitchell's husband, Donnie.

"It was a real easy delivery," Mitchell said, adding that her labor pains were eased by a local anesthetic. "In between pushing we were laughing and having a good time. … I felt guilty."

Mitchell had given birth to four children during her first marriage; they range in age from 21 to 32. She and her current husband adopted a child four years ago, but she said she didn't want to adopt another because adoption officials have too much control over the process.

The in-vitro process "put me in total control," she said. "It was so easy. I knew I could do it."

Mitchell said being pregnant in her 50s posed few problems, although some of her close friends were concerned because it "changed the relationship" among them. Most of her peers, along with her family members, were supportive, she said.

"Scientists are studying the health risks incurred by pregnant women in their 50s," said endocrinologist Mark Sauer, who implanted the embryo in Mitchell's uterus at USC. The cost of the implant is about $10,000.

Of ten women in their 50s who have participated in USC's in-vitro fertilization program, he said four have gotten pregnant, including Mitchell. Three delivered successfully. The fourth had a miscarriage.

To sustain her pregnancy, Mitchell received hormone supplements for 100 days, hospital officials said. Mitchell said she is able to nurse the baby, but does not plan to do so.

Mitchell's obstetrician and gynecologist, Kathryn Shaw, said her patient's history of easy deliveries prepared her for the latest birth. "It went very well," Shaw said.

Mitchell, a country and western singer who operates the Ban Dar nightclub in Ventura with her former husband, Jim Shields, said she expects to return to work as soon as she gets back in shape.

COMPREHENSION QUESTIONS

1. Could Mrs. Mitchell have had this baby without the aid of in-vitro fertilization? Why or why not?

2. Why didn't the Mitchells choose to adopt another child?

3. What do you think Mrs. Mitchell meant when she said that some of her friends were worried that her pregnancy "changed the relationship" among them?

IN YOUR OPINION

1. This article shows that even the physical condition of menopause is no longer a barrier to pregnancy. How do you feel about medical technology changing a woman's ability to have children?

2. Technological advances such as the one described in this article make the idea of an actual "test tube baby," that is, a baby grown completely outside of a human body, seem possible in the near future. Do you think scientific experimentation concerning the creation of human life,

which could lead to true "test tube babies," is a good direction for science to follow? Why or why not?

_____

_____

RELATED READING: MORE TRENDS CONCERNING THE AMERICAN FAMILY

Read the article *Changes in the "Traditional" American Family* and answer the questions that follow.

Changes in the "Traditional" American Family

The U.S. government is interested in trends that affect the American family. To investigate how families are changing, every ten years the U.S. Census Bureau collects data on all U.S. households. From the information it receives, the bureau examines such important aspects of American life as family size and composition. It can then compare its findings with the results of the censuses taken in the past to identify trends in the American family.

Information from a sample of 57,400 households surveyed by the Census Bureau in March of 1990 indicates that the "traditional" American family—a family consisting of two parents and children under the age of 18—is on the decline. The "traditional" family made up only 40 percent of U.S. households in 1970, 31 percent in 1980, and 26 percent in the year 1990. The more than 70 percent of households falling outside of the category "traditional" family includes households consisting of never-married parents and children, divorced parents and children, couples without children, parents and children over 18 years of age, people living alone, and unrelated adults living in the same household.

Findings of this survey reveal other interesting trends in American family life. One finding was that while the rate of divorce and childbirth out of wedlock (involving couples not married) continued to increase, both of these phenomena increased at a slower pace during the 1980s than during the previous decade. But the number of unmarried couples living together appears to be increasing rapidly, with the number in the 1990 survey showing an 80 percent increase over the number in 1980. The long-term general trend toward smaller families was shown to continue, with the size of the average American household dropping, from 3.67 people in 1940, to 3.14 in 1970, to 2.76 in 1980, to a low of 2.63 in 1990.

COMPREHENSION QUESTIONS

1. What does the "traditional" American family consist of?

_____

_____

2. What did the 1990 Census Bureau survey reveal about the "traditional" American family?

_____

_____

3. According to the 1990 survey, what percentage of U.S. families in the did NOT fall into the "traditional" family category?

_____

_____

4. What are some examples of households that fall outside of the category "traditional" family ?

_____

_____

5. List at least four other trends that the survey revealed about U.S. family life.

_____

_____

GROUP DISCUSSION QUESTIONS

1. What does a "traditional" family in your own culture consist of?
2. In what ways is family life changing in your own culture?
3. Are any of the trends taking place in U.S. family life similar to trends taking place in your own culture? If so, which ones?
4. Which trends noted in the reading, if any, are different from trends in your own culture? What reasons can you suggest for the differences?

FINAL TEAM TASK: CONDUCTING YOUR OWN SURVEY

Now you will have the opportunity to find out about the kinds of families that your class as a group comes from by conducting your own surveys.

1. Form groups of 3–5 members. Each group will conduct its own survey.

2. In your groups, make a list of questions about the nature of the family. For example: How many children were in your family? At what age did you move from your parents' home? Try to have at least six questions.

3. Collect data on all of the members of your class, including the members of your own group, by having everyone fill out a survey. Be sure that no one puts his or her name on the survey since surveys look only at group rather than individual data.

4. Analyze the data your group collected by turning the responses on your survey into numbers. Example: 20 percent of the members of this class moved away from home when they were in their 20s.

5. Present the results of your survey orally to the rest of the class.

FINAL WRITTEN TASK

OPTION A

Write a two-paragraph summary of the survey you conducted.

1. In the first paragraph give general information about the topic of the survey: how many questions were asked, how many people responded, and who the people were. Do not give the people's names, just some general information about them.
2. In the second paragraph give more specific information about the results of the survey.

OPTION B

Write a short paper (one or two pages) comparing and contrasting changes taking place in U.S. family life with changes in family life that are taking place in your own culture.

Segment 2

Fast-Track Parents

from *Business World*, 5/7/89
Runtime: 4:43
Begin: 16:01

Previewing

KEY QUESTIONS

1. What professions are high-prestige?
2. What is important to people who want to have a high-prestige, high income job in a short amount of time?
3. What are the effects on children of both parents' having a career?

DISCUSSION

1. The video segment is about parents who have "fast-track" jobs: top executive, sales, or managerial positions. What are some of the personality characteristics of people who hold such jobs?

_____

_____

2. Why do you think people want to have fast-track jobs?

_____

_____

3. Would you want a fast-track job? Why or why not?

_____

_____

4. What are some of the positive and negative aspects of both parents in a family having fast-track jobs?

_____

_____

PREDICTION

Based on the title of this segment, *Fast-Track Parents*, the discussion you've had with your classmates, and your own knowledge, what information do you think will be included in this video segment?

1. _____

2. _____

3. _____

4. _____

Note: After you have watched the entire segment once, come back to this section and confirm your predictions by circling any that were correct.

ESSENTIAL WORDS TO KNOW

The *italicized* words are from this video segment. Use the context clues in the sentences below to help you understand the meaning of the words. Write your own definition for each word. Then discuss your definitions with the class.

1. One *subculture* in American society which is growing rapidly is the family in which both parents have high-power, high-salary positions that require them to work very long hours.
   subculture: _____

2. Most people desire a job with an *income* that will allow them to live comfortably.
   income: _____

3. While this situation is not entirely new, the family with two fast-track parents is more common than ever before, now that *baby boomers* are at the peak of their wage-earning years.
   baby boomers: _____

4. Fast-track parents usually have quite high *expectations* for themselves.
   expectations: _____

5. Parents who have fast-track jobs might also hope their children live up to their own *high standards*.

   high standards: _____

Global Viewing

GETTING THE MAIN IDEAS

Watch the entire video segment and circle the best answer to each question.

00:16:20-
00:20:25

1. What is said about the two career parents in this video?
   a. They love their jobs.
   b. They work very long hours.
   c. They don't like caring for their child.
   d. Both a and b.

2. Which of the following statements is NOT said about fast-track parents?
   a. They are part of the baby-boomer generation.
   b. They are highly intelligent.
   c. They are a growing segment of the U.S. population.
   d. They want to provide good lives for their children.

3. What concern do some people have about fast-track parents?
   a. Their long work hours are bad for their health.
   b. Their children will be spoiled.
   c. Their children will feel too much pressure to succeed.
   d. None of the above.

4. What has been done to avoid some of the negative effects that have occurred in families with two fast-track parents?
   a. Psychiatrists have convinced one parent to slow down his or her career.
   b. Fast-track parents have given their children money to make up for the lack of time they spend together.
   c. The children have gone to psychiatrists to get emotional help.
   d. Some schools have tried to lessen the pressure on children by getting rid of grades.

5. Which of the following is NOT what the children of fast-track parents need?
   a. More material things from their parents.
   b. More attention from their parents.
   c. More time spent with their parents.
   d. All of the above.

Intensive Viewing

LISTENING FOR IMPORTANT INFORMATION

00:17:16-
00:18:30

Watch this part of the segment and put a *P* next to the personality traits listed below that are mentioned as traits often found in fast-track parents. Put a *C* next to the traits that are mentioned in regard to the children of fast-track parents. Leave a blank after the traits that are not mentioned in the video segment.

_____	1. anxious	_____	5. relaxed
_____	2. intelligent	_____	6. competitive
_____	3. perfect	_____	7. perfectionist
_____	4. have high standards for themselves	_____	8. driven

LISTENING CLOZE

00:17:16-
00:18:33

Watch this part of the segment and fill in the blanks with the missing words. Then compare answers with those of another student.

Sander Vanocur: They are fast-trackers, part of a growing _____ of wealth.

Andree Brooks: Fast-track parents are, first of all, fast-track people. They are _____. They are very often _____. They expect very high standards from themselves, and, in a way, all those traits they expect also from their children.

Sander Vanocur: Of the more than two million households nationwide with a reported _____ of $100,000 or more, one-quarter, 500,000, have at least one dependent child. And in about half of those households, both parents work in fast-track jobs—top executive professional, sales or managerial positions. It's a _____ segment that's increased 76 percent in just five years. From Fairfield County, Connecticut, to California, they, like all _____ , share a desire to provide the best for their children in the nicest setting. And these parents expect the best from their children in return. The constant _____ to perform carries a high emotional cost.

Nicholas Thatcher: We see children who are _____. We see children who are more competitive than the sorts of natural _____ that is developmentally inherent in children.

GETTING THE DETAILS

First read the questions below. Then watch this part of the segment and take notes. When you've finished, compare your notes with those of another student.

00:19:00-
00:20:25

1. Who does Sheldon Zablow, the child psychiatrist, compare the children of fast-track parents to?

   _____

   _____

2. Why are fast-track children similar to this group of children?

   _____

   _____

3. What does Bill say about the kind of profession he is in?

   _____

   _____

4. What does Stephanie say is the easiest thing about her work?

   _____

   _____

5. What does Stephanie say is the hardest thing about her work?

   _____

   _____

6. What does Bill say is a risk of being on the fast track?

   _____

   _____

Language Focus

UNDERSTANDING IDIOMS

Read the sentences below and try to define the *italicized* idioms. Then discuss your definitions with the class.

1. To work at a fast-track job, you have to *put in long hours*.

   put in long hours: _____

2. *The bottom line is* that no material possessions or fancy homes can provide children with the one thing they need most—time with their parents.

   the bottom line _____

3. Today most parents have to face the problem of *juggling a career and children*.

   juggling a career and children: _____

4. Max said he likes to see his mother *boss people around*.

   boss people around: _____

EXPANDING YOUR VOCABULARY

The words and phrases below are all related to the topic of the video segment. Write each word or phrase under the definition in the chart that is closest in meaning.

bring up a child   have a baby   babysit

rear a child   care for a baby   bear a child

look after a child   become a parent   raise a child

GIVE BIRTH TO A BABY	TAKE CARE OF A CHILD TEMPORARILY	BE RESPONSIBLE FOR A CHILD UNTIL THE CHILD IS GROWN UP

VOCABULARY CHECK

The sentences below are from the video segment. Match the *italicized* words and expressions with their equivalents from the list.

a. natural   d. victim

b. without limits   e. attractive quality

c. highest level

_____ 1. With baby boomers now in their *peak* earning years, how would their expectations affect the next generation?

_____ 2. We see children who are more competitive than the sorts of natural competition that is developmentally *inherent* in children.

_____ 3. Bill and Stephanie have seen enough of the pressure of the fast track to know they don't want Max to fall *prey* to it.

_____ 4. But, they admit the lifestyle has its *lure*.

_____ 5. I am in a profession where there is no limitation on how much growth you can create for yourself and perhaps how much money you can make or . . . It is almost *boundless*.

Postviewing

COMPARING CULTURES

Discuss the following questions in small groups.

1. Were you surprised or shocked by anything you learned from this video?
2. What do you think are some of the social changes that have occurred since the beginning of the U.S. baby-boom generation that have contributed to the phenomenon of fast-track parents?
3. Can you imagine what the children of fast-track parents might be like when they become adults? What might be some of their positive and negative personality traits?
4. Does a "fast-track parent" trend exist in your country? If so, what is your reaction to it? If not, why do you think this trend is occurring in some parts of the world, but not in your country?
5. Can you imagine yourself raising a family in which both you and your spouse (husband or wife) have fast-track careers? If so, what would you do to ensure that your children do not suffer from some of the pressures mentioned in the video?

RELATED READING: BABY BOOMER TRENDS

In addition to the subculture examined in the video segment *Fast-Track Parents,* the last decade has seen the rise (and fall) of two other groups. Read the following article to prepare for the discussion questions that follow.

Yuppies

Meet John Smith at 24 years old. After recently receiving his MBA from Harvard, he's already earning twice as much as his father as a financial analyst for a major east coast investment firm. Like many of his colleagues, he's young, lives in an urban environment, and has a professional position in a successful, growing company — in other words, John fits the yuppie profile. Let's follow him through a typical day.

7:00 a.m.: The alarm jolts him out of bed at the same time the Braun automatic coffeemaker kicks on in the kitchen. He jumps in the shower, shaves, rips open one of the half-dozen boxes of freshly laundered white shirts waiting on the shelf, finishes dressing, and pours a cup of coffee. He sits down to a piece of whole wheat toast while he flips through the *Wall Street Journal.* By 7:15, briefcase in one hand, gym bag in the other, he's out the door and in the BMW, ready to start the day.

7:45 a.m.: Seated at his desk, eyes glued to the spread sheet displayed on the PC monitor in front of him, he prepares for the hours of phone calls and meetings that occupy his mornings.

Noon: At the health club down the street from his office, John strips off the charcoal gray suit and changes into his t-shirt, shorts, and the latest in designer running shoes for a fast-paced game of racquet ball. Then on to the club dining room where he has scheduled lunch with a potential client. They discuss business over sparkling water and pasta, and a cappuccino tops off the meal.

2:30 p.m.: Caffeine coursing through John's system, he's now eager for several more hours of frantic meetings and phone calls.

6:00 p.m.: John phones out for delivery of dinner from the gourmet deli down the block to keep him going through the next two to three hours he'll spend at his desk.

10:00 p.m.: He gets home just in time to sit down to a bowl of frozen yogurt and a rerun of this season's most popular drama series before turning in.

A schedule such as this doesn't allow a lot of time for nonwork-related pleasures that other people John's age tend to seek out, such as romance. This does seem to be one of the hazards of the yuppie lifestyle. But, given a few years, John may find an equally ambitious mate. If John and his mate decide to have children and continue their fast-paced careers, they will then face the problems of many fast-track parents. They could, however, decide that children don't fit into their hectic schedules. In this case, John and his spouse would become part of another cultural trend that has grown throughout the 1980s.

Dinks

This group is among the favorites of marketing experts. With dual incomes and no kids, couples in this category have an abundance of discretionary income. While the saying. "Two can live as cheaply as one" is not completely true, two sources of incomes and only one apartment to rent mean that there's more left to spend at the end of the month.

What *do* Dinks choose to spend this disposable income on? Look around as you walk down the street in any upscale, urban neighborhood. Count the number of fancy pet accessory stores and veterinarian's offices. Without children, dogs or cats often become the recipients of lavish gifts and attention. Dinks give to their pets' diet the same careful thought they give to their own daily nutritional needs. In addition to the dozens of brands of dog and cat food available in the average grocery store, an almost equal number of "designer" health food brands is available in pet stores — one kind for the growing kitten or puppy, another for the young adult, and a low-calorie version for the "mature" cat or dog.

How do couples with such demanding jobs have time to prepare their own meals to come home to? The number of restaurants and gourmet take-out delis in between the pet accessory stores and veterinarian's offices provide a clue. Restaurateurs keep up with the latest food manias, and while the take-out food choices of the '60s were limited to pizza, chow mein, or McDonalds, the number of options exploded in the 1980s. Any ethnic variety as well as the latest health food fad can be taken home hot and ready to eat or, even better, delivered to your door with a video to watch with your meal.

To get an idea of the other ways Dinks spend their money and free time, pick up some of the magazines on the rack at an upscale neighborhood gym. The advertisements will give a good idea of how you, too, could spend disposable income provided by two salaries and only two of the people to spend them on.

GROUP DISCUSSION QUESTIONS

1. The lifestyles of yuppies and dinks are outlined above, but the values or goals that members of these two subcultures might have are not directly stated. What goals and values do you think are associated with the yuppie and dink lifestyle?

2. Do either of the two subcultures, yuppies or dinks, exist in your culture? If so, discuss the characteristics you associate with either of these groups as they exist in your own culture.

3. These two social phenomena, yuppies and dinks, are products of the 1980s. In what ways do they differ from the typical lifestyle of young people of your parents' generation? Use the chart below to make comparisons.

	PARENT'S GENERATION	YUPPIES & DINKS
INCOME		
WORK		
LEISURE		
VALUES		

MINI-RESEARCH TASK

In the 1960s a way of life that became known as the hippie lifestyle developed. This lifestyle was associated with a certain philosophy about work, relationships, family, and other established institutions as well as with a specific style of dress and appearance. The 1980s produced the yuppie lifestyle, which also had its particular philosophy, values, and fashion.

1. Read about these two lifestyles in books, magazines, or newspapers and take notes on what you read.
2. Use your notes to give an oral report to the class. Include in your report:
   a. a summary of the information in the articles you read
   b. three discussion questions for the class. These should NOT be comprehension questions that ask for a factual response, but subjective questions that stimulate a class discussion.

FINAL TEAM TASK: ROLE PLAY

Work in groups of 3 or 4. All of you are in a radio interview about the consequences of the fast-track family lifestyle. Each student will play one of the roles described on page 23. Read the situation and role descriptions on page 23 and decide who will play each role. Prepare for ten minutes before beginning the interview.

The Situation: A Radio Interview

The number of U.S. families in which both parents work in fast-track jobs has increased approximately 75 percent over the last five years. Such an increase has created a subculture of families that has some people — from teachers to child psychiatrists — concerned. A popular radio talk show interviewer has made fast-track parents and their children the topic of today's most listened-to show.

Role Description: Interviewer

You are the most popular radio talk show host on the air today. Your interview style, in which you encourage the interview subjects to become angry and argue with each other on the air, is what accounts for your popularity. The questions you ask are often intended to cause your subjects to get involved in heated arguments.

Role Description: Fast-Track Parent

You are the mother or father of a five-year-old child. You and your spouse spend an average of 60 hours a week at the office, as well as bringing work home with you several evenings a week and on the weekend. In addition to earning a six-figure salary, you love your work and find it to be one of the most rewarding aspects of your life. You are proud that you can afford to send your child to the most prestigious kindergarten in your city. One of the best aspects of this kindergarten is that it also provides after-school day care until 9:00 p.m. for those evenings when you just can't get away from the office.

Role Description: Child of Fast-Track Parent

Although you are very proud of your parents, you are sometimes jealous of the other children in your class whose mother or father picks them up at 3:00 p.m. while you often wait for a parent until 9:00 p.m. You sometimes brag to your classmates about the latest toy you received from your parents, and sometimes your bragging and competitive nature cause you to start fights with other kids in the class.

Role Description: Child Psychiatrist

In the past your patients were often children between the ages of six and sixteen whose parents were divorced. Recently, you have noticed that an increasing number of your patients are children from affluent, upper-class homes with two professional parents. It's remarkable to you that some of the same symptoms of children of divorce show up in children from these families. The children often seem to have received too little parental attention, and are aggressive and overly competitive, because of this.

FINAL WRITTEN TASK

Choose either Option A or Option B below and write a four-paragraph essay in which you compare and contrast two lifestyles. Use the following format to write your essay:

1. In the introductory paragraph explain what you will be comparing and give some general background information about each subject of comparison.
2. In the second paragraph describe the essential characteristics of one of the subjects of comparison.
3. In the third paragraph describe the essential characteristics of the other subject of comparison.
4. In the concluding paragraph summarize the similarities and differences between the two subjects. Expand on your summary by adding a brief explanation of why you believe these differences exist.

OPTION A

Compare and contrast the yuppie/dink lifestyle and the lifestyle of people in your parents' generation.

OPTION B

Compare and contrast the hippie lifestyle with that of the yuppie/dink lifestyle.

Segment 3

Is Love Color-blind?

from *20/20*, 8/13/87
Runtime: 20:49
Begin 20:52

Previewing

KEY QUESTIONS

1. Do children of minority ethnic groups face problems when adopted by white families?
2. Why would people want to adopt a child whose ethnic heritage differs from their own?
3. Does transracial adoption threaten the survival of minority ethnic groups?

DISCUSSION

1. Do transracial adoptions take place in your country? Are there problems associated with mixed-race or mixed ethnic families formed by such adoptions? If so, what kind of problems?

_____

_____

2. Do you think there should be legal guidelines that limit transracial adoptions?

_____

_____

PREDICTION

Based on the title of the segment, *Is Love Color-blind?*, the key questions, and your own background knowledge, what do you think you will see and hear on the video? Write down four items under each of the headings below. Confirm your predictions after you have watched the entire segment once.

SIGHTS (THINGS YOU EXPECT TO SEE)	WORDS (WORDS YOU EXPECT TO HEAR)
1. _____	_____
2. _____	_____
3. _____	_____
4. _____	_____

ESSENTIAL WORDS TO KNOW

The *italicized* words in the sentences below are all used in the video. Read the sentences and then match the words or expressions with their meanings from the list.

a. having a serious physical or mental disability
b. unreasonable dislike of someone or something
c. a social rule that some words, subjects or actions must be avoided because they are embarrassing or offensive
d. a situation in which adults officially take a child into their family for a period of time without becoming the child's legal parents
e. qualities and traditions that have continued over many generations
f. involving people of different races

_____ 1. There has been a gradual lifting of the *taboo* on talking about the war.

_____ 2. Until fairly recently, *transracial* marriages were against the law in South Africa.

_____ 3. The little girl was in *foster care* for six years before she was legally adopted.

_____ 4. Community leaders would like to see more effective action taken against racial *prejudice*.

_____ 5. In spite of being seriously *handicapped*, he managed to live a full and rewarding life.

_____ 6. She was very proud of her cultural *heritage*.

Global Viewing

GETTING THE MAIN IDEAS

Read the following sentences. Then watch the entire video segment and check (✔) the sentences that are true. Compare your answers with those of another student.

_____ 1. Transracial adoption is becoming a major issue in the United States.

_____ 2. State courts and social welfare agencies in the U.S. place too much priority on adoption and not enough on foster care.

_____ 3. In the U.S., relatively few minority children are in foster care.

_____ 4. Black social workers and Native Americans are opposed to transracial adoption.

_____ 5. More and more couples are adopting minority children because of the limited availability of healthy, young white children.

_____ 6. Most of the children in foster homes are not being adopted because of their race.

Intensive Viewing

LISTENING CLOZE

Watch this part of the segment and fill in the blanks with the missing words. Then compare your answers with those of another student.

Hugh Downs: Tonight, a love story, a story of _____ who want children so much that they're willing to _____ breaking what some feel are social _____ to adopt children across racial and _____ lines. Transracial adoption is becoming a _____ issue in the United States, and we think it's so _____ that first, we want you to understand what's prompting more and more people to advocate _____ adoption as a solution to a growing problem, and that's the problem of _____ - term foster care.

GETTING THE FIGURES

Watch the next part of the segment and fill in the blanks in the statements below with the missing numbers.

1. In the United States, _____ out of every ten children in foster care are minority kids.

27

2. About _____ children are in the foster care system.
3. Only about _____ of the children in foster care have been legally freed for adoption.

LISTENING FOR DETAILS

Watch this part of the segment and chose the best answer to each question.

00:28:18-
00:37:00

1. According to Hugh Downs, why is there increasing pressure for transracial adoption?
   a. Because it is no longer a social taboo in the United States.
   b. Because minority children are in the foster care in disproportionately large numbers.
   c. Because so many handicapped children need to be adopted.
   d. Both a and b.

2. Why is the National Association of Black Social Workers against transracial adoption?
   a. They want black children to preserve their ethnic identity.
   b. They feel black children can learn to function better in American society if they are brought up in a black family.
   c. They feel that black children will not be treated kindly in white families.
   d. Both a and b.

3. Which of the following is NOT true about Mrs. Bialack?
   a. Her adopted daughter, Amanda, is half Hispanic.
   b. She and her husband got Amanda through a county adoption clinic.
   c. She feels the county rules about the ethnic matching of children and families are too rigid.
   d. She feels angry about adoption rules.

4. According to Leora Neal, why won't most of the children in foster homes benefit from transracial adoption?
   a. Because most of them are older.
   b. Because many of them are handicapped.
   c. Because a large percentage of them are male.
   d. Both a and b.

5. Which statement about Mark and Chris Shearer is true?
   a. They were both adopted by a white family when they were infants.
   b. They are both glad they grew up where they did.
   c. They both have an identity problem.
   d. They both learned about current black culture growing up in a white home.

6. According to Stone Phillips, what is the main issue in the debate over transracial adoption?
   a. Whether minority families who want to adopt should should have to compete with whites for children of their own race.
   b. Whether kids are better off with parents of the same race.
   c. Whether placing minority kids with white families is preferable to leaving them in institutional shelters or foster homes.
   d. Whether transracial adoption is actually a kind of cultural genocide.

7. Which of the following is NOT true about the court case involving Baby Ashley?
   a. Ruth Robbins and her husband had already signed the adoption papers when Jana Neu decided she wanted to keep the baby.
   b. The Neus had been Baby Ashley's foster parents when she was an infant.
   c. It was the first case in which a transracial adoption was suggested.
   d. The court decided in favor of Jana Neu.

8. When did Clara Barksdale adopt Marian?
   a. Eighteen years ago.
   b. When Marian was an adolescent.
   c. After Marian went into therapy.
   d. After Marian had spent several years as her foster child.

9. Which of the following problems did Marian experience in adolescence?
   a. She began to feel uncomfortable when she was with her father.
   b. Other kids called her insulting names like "oreo" or "nigger."
   c. She did not identify with her mother.
   d. Both a and b.

10. Which of the following is NOT true about Clara Barksdale?
   a. She was prepared to deal with the problems that occurred when Marian became an adolescent.
   b. She thinks it's important for agencies to encourage minority families to adopt.
   c. She feels that the worst times are over because Marian is now stronger.
   d. Both a and b.

LISTENING FOR IMPORTANT INFORMATION

Watch this part of the segment and take brief notes on the answers to the questions below. Then compare your notes with those of another student. If you disagree, watch the segment again.

1. What does the One Church, One Child program do to encourage minority adoption?

   _____

   _____

2. How many teenage boys did Father George Clements adopt? How many families in his parish have adopted black children?

   _____

   _____

3. How long does it take the Illinois DCFS (Department of Children and Family Services) to place a child for adoption? How long did it take before Father Clements started the One Church, One Child program?

   _____

   _____

4. According to Gordon Johnson, what two things are responsible for the success of the Illinois DCFS in placing children for adoption?

   _____

   _____

5. According to Stone Phillips, why aren't the thousands of kids in foster homes being adopted?

   _____

   _____

6. What has the National Adoption Center in Philadelphia done to help kids in foster homes get adopted?

   _____

   _____

Language Focus

STATING A PERSONAL OPINION

On the video segment, Maggie Bialack states a personal opinion when she says, "*I believe that* Eddie and I are the best possible adoptive parents for Amanda."

Here are four common ways of stating a personal opinion:

a. I believe (that) . . .
c. I think (that) . . .
b. I feel (that) . . .
d. In my opinion, . . .

State a personal opinion about each of the following topics. Introduce each opinion with expression *a, b, c,* or *d* as indicated. Look at the example.

> State a personal opinion about the court's decision to let Baby Ashley stay with a white family. (d)
>
> *In my opinion*, the court made the right decision.

1. State a personal opinion about transracial adoptions. (b)

   _____

   _____

2. State a personal opinion about the importance of preserving children's ethnic identity. (a)

   _____

   _____

3. State a personal opinion about the potential problems in transracial adoptions. (c)

   _____

   _____

4. State a personal opinion about parents who adopt children of another race. (d)

   _____

   _____

5. State a personal opinion about the One Church, One Child adoption program. (c)

   _____

   _____

SUPPORTING YOUR OPINION

In the video, Leora Neal states and then supports an opinion when she says, "In 1972, the National Association of Black Social Workers took a stand against transracial placements *for a variety of reasons. Number one*, we were concerned that the ethnic identity of the black child be preserved . . ."

Here are four common, but rather formal, ways of supporting a personal opinion.

a. (Opinion stated) *for a variety of reasons. Number one, . . .*
b. (Opinion stated). *We have found that . . .*
c. (Opinion stated). *A study by X has found that . . .*
d. *Given the fact that . . ., (opinion stated).*

Work in pairs. Ask each other the following questions. When answering, support your opinion using expression *a, b, c,* or *d* as indicated. Look at the example below.

> Question: Are you in favor of transracial adoption ? (a)
>
> Response: Yes. I believe that transracial adoptions should be allowed for a variety of reasons. Number one, there is a higher percentage of children from minority ethnic groups living in foster homes. Number two, . . .

1. Question: Do you think transracial adoptions should be allowed ? (b)

   Response: _____

   _____

2. Question: Do you feel it is important to preserve a child's ethnic identity? (c)

   Response: _____

   _____.

3. Question: Do you think the parents' desire to nurture, love, and raise an infant will make up for the problems the child of a transracial adoption might face growing up? (a)

   Response: _____

   _____

4. Question: Do you think that the One Church, One Child program is beneficial? (d)

   Response: _____

Postviewing

COMPARING CULTURES

Discuss the following questions in small groups.

1. Were you surprised or shocked by anything you learned from this video?
2. The United States is a country of many different ethnic groups. Why do you think that the arguments given against transracial adoption were stated the most strongly by people who represented ethnic groups that are minorities in the United States?
3. It was said in this video that many people who adopt infants whose ethnic heritage is different from their own are thinking only of their personal need for nurturing a baby. They are not thinking of what problems this will create for the adopted child later in life. How do you feel about this point of view?
4. Because it has become so difficult for white American couples to adopt healthy infants, there is a trend for private adoption agencies to arrange for U.S. couples to adopt infants from other countries. What do you think of this trend?
5. Do some of the same problems discussed in the video concerning transracial adoption occur in your country? Why or why not?
6. Does your country have other problems associated with adoption that were not mentioned in this video segment? If so, what are some of these problems?

RELATED READING: GATHERING THE EVIDENCE

The following paragraphs contain information about some of the issues involved in the transracial controversy. Work in groups. Read each paragraph and decide whether it includes evidence *for* or *against* transracial adoption. Then write a sentence (or two) that summarizes the evidence. In some cases, the evidence could be used to support either side of the issue.

1. Chris Shearer, who appeared in the video segment you saw, is a young black adult who was raised in a white family since infancy. He has experienced difficulty establishing a sense of identity. "I've always really had an identity crisis because, you know. I'm not really black, but I'm not really white. And so, I've always kind of been just in the middle, you know, between people." He expresses some dissatisfaction about having been brought up in a white culture. He says "There's this new breed of professionals, black people I've been meeting. And they seem

to have really high goals." He wishes that he could have had some exposure to this aspect of black culture while he was growing up.

_____

_____

2. An 18-year study was carried out by Rita Simon of American University and Howard Altstein of the University of Maryland. The researchers studied 386 minority children who had been adopted by 200 white families. The data they collected indicated that children adopted into interracial families did not seem to have problems concerning their sense of security or any other specific psychological problems. According to Simon, "Transracial adoption . . . may, in fact, produce black, white, and Asian adults with special interpersonal talents and skills at bridging cultures."

_____

_____

3. It has been claimed that a black child brought up in a white home will face difficult problems when he or she leaves home to enter the real world. The claim is that such a child will encounter rejection by both black and white culture: rejection by the white world because of the color of his or her skin, and rejection by the black world due to his or her "white" values and behavior. Such an experience could result in serious psychological harm.

_____

_____

4. The term "cultural genocide" has been used to refer to situations in which whites are given custody of minority children. Members of both black and Native American communities have feared that transracial adoption threatens their cultural survival. This fear was a major factor in bringing about the 1978 Indian Child Welfare Act, which was enacted to ensure the survival of the Native American culture. Before this legal measure was passed, studies conducted in the late 1960s and early 1970s found that "between 25% and 35% of American Indian children were placed in institutions or in adoptive or foster care. . . " (as reported in *Time*, May 2, 1988, p.64) and most were placed with non-Indian families.

_____

_____

5. Clara Barksdale, the Hispanic adoptive mother of a black daughter, says that although her daughter identifies strongly with her, at times she has felt helpless when her daughter has faced racial discrimination. She wonders whether she can help Marian cope with some of the more painful situations that will come about because of her skin color. "And how can I really help her if I did not experience that myself?" she asks.

_____

_____

6. Ruth McRoy of the University of Texas conducted a study in which she compared two groups of black middle-class teenagers. The teenagers in one group had been adopted by black families, while those in the other group had been adopted by white families. In the results she found no difference in the self-esteem of the members of the two groups; she did, however, note differences in the teenagers' perception of their racial identity. One area in which this difference was evident was in dating and marriage. Those teenagers who had been brought up in black families tended to date and want to marry other blacks. The group raised by white parents had a tendency to minimize racial difference as an important factor in choosing a mate.

_____

_____

FINAL TEAM TASK: DEBATING THE ISSUE

Divide the class into two teams: Pro and Con. Conduct a debate on the controversy surrounding transracial adoption. In your team do the following:

1. Each team member will choose one of the following roles below to play in arguing the team's case.
   - a social worker who works with adopted children
   - a psychologist who has treated adopted children or adolescents
   - a professor who has conducted research in the area of transracial adoption
   - an adoptive parent of a child from a different ethnic background
   - an adopted minority child or adolescent
2. Choose a moderator who will be neutral, that is, she will not argue for either side.
3. Read the background description for your side. Do NOT read the background description for the other team.

4. Prepare an argument approximately three minutes long for the debate.
5. Follow the procedure below when conducting the debate:
   A. The Pro team begins with a three-minute presentation.
   B. The Con team then gives a three-minute presentation.
   C. The Pro team gives a three-minute response to the Con team's presentation.
   D. The Con team gives a three-minute response to the Pro team's presentation.
   E. The moderator summarizes and evaluates the strengths of both arguments.

PRO TEAM

You will present a legal policy that is pro (for) transracial adoption. Consider the following issues in preparing your arguments:

- the long-term foster care situation in which over 275,000 children spend their childhood
- the right of childless couples to fulfill their desire to have a family
- the psychological importance of family stability and love

CON TEAM

You will present a legal policy that is con (against) transracial adoption. Consider the following issues in preparing your arguments:

- the importance of self-identity, which develops throughout childhood and adolescence
- the need for minority groups to maintain their cultural identity
- the fact that many children who end up in long-term foster care are not healthy infants and would probably not be adopted even if transracial adoptions were allowed

FINAL WRITTEN TASK

Write a 3–5 paragraph essay in which you express your opinion about transracial adoption.

1. In the first paragraph introduce the issue of transracial adoption and state in one sentence what your opinion on this issue is.
2. In the second through fourth paragraphs support your opinion with evidence to show the reader the reasons for your beliefs.
3. In the final paragraph write a conclusion in which you briefly summarize your evidence and write a strong concluding statement to back up your opinion.

Segment 4

Manufacturers Engage in False Advertising on the Environment

from *World News Tonight*, 5/14/91
Runtime: 5:03
Begin: 41:45

Previewing

KEY QUESTIONS

1. What is the manufacturer's motive in making claims about the environmental safety of its products?
2. Are consumers satisfied with the information they receive in commercials that make environmental claims?
3. Should national guidelines monitor the claims made by manufacturers about the environmental safety of their products?

DISCUSSION

1. Do manufacturers in your country make claims about the environmental safety of their products? If so, what claims do they make about the products?

_____

_____

2. As a consumer do you pay attention to claims a manufacturer makes on the packaging or in advertising about the environmental safety of a product? Do such claims influence your choice of products?

_____

_____

UNIT 2 WORK IN AMERICA

3. Tell about a specific incident in which environmental claims influenced your decision to buy a product.

_____

_____

PREDICTION

The title indicates that the topic of this video segment will include claims made by manufacturers about their products. List some products and the environmental claims you predict will be made about them. Confirm your predictions after you have watched the entire segment once.

	PRODUCTS	ENVIRONMENTAL CLAIMS
1.	_____	_____
2.	_____	_____
3.	_____	_____
4.	_____	_____

ESSENTIAL WORDS TO KNOW

The *italicized* words in the sentences below are all used in the video. Read the sentences and then match the words or expressions with their meanings from the list.

a. confusing; leading in the wrong direction
b. customer interest in buying products which that harm the environment
c. a group formed to study a specific problem and offer a solution
d. made from an already existing product
e. work that involves studying the interests and habits of consumers
f. able to break down and decompose naturally

_____ 1. Industries do *market research* to find out what consumers are interested in buying.

_____ 2. After conducting surveys of consumer interests, industries have found that *green consumerism* is an important trend in buying habits.

_____ 3. Products made from *degradable* ingredients don't add a lot of waste to the environment.

_____ 4. Many paper products are made from *recycled* materials.

_____ 5. He said the information in the report was both false and *misleading*.

_____ 6. The government has set up a *task force* on air pollution.

Global Viewing

00:41:59-
00:46:22

TEAM COMPETITION

1. Form small groups of 3–5 people and number the groups I, II, III, etc.
2. After watching the video segment, discuss it with the members of your group. Together make up five questions about the ideas discussed in the video segment to ask other teams. Have a representative of your group write down the questions and have your team members check the questions to make sure that they are logical, well-formed sentences.
3. The competition begins with a member from Group I asking a member from Group II a question. If the question is answered correctly, Group II gets a point. Then Group II asks a question of Group III, and so on.

QUESTIONS

1. _____

2. _____

3. _____

4. _____

5. _____

Intensive Viewing

00:41:59-
00:42:28

LISTENING CLOZE

Watch this part of the segment and fill in the blanks with the missing words. Then compare your answers with those of another student.

Peter Jennings: We put the environment on the American Agenda tonight, and what we hope to do is make some sense out of a subject that is confusing to many of us. The number of _____ products on the market which claim to be good for the environment or at least _____ safe has increased enormously. Manufacturers read their _____ _____, and they know that a majority of Americans prefer to do business with companies that do not damage the world around us. It's called _____ _____. The trouble is so much of the _____ and the packaging is downright _____.

39

LISTENING FOR DETAILS

Watch this part of the segment and circle the best answer to each question.

1. What did DuPont say that its energy unit would do to safeguard the environment?
    a. Use cleaner methods for refining its oil.
    b. Use double-hulled oil tankers.
    c. Save the planet.
    d. Both a and b.

2. What are some methods used by giant corporations to suggest that their company is environmentally friendly?
    a. They train seals to applaud themselves.
    b. They hire celebrities.
    c. They sign up for environmental causes.
    d. Both a and b.

3. According to consumer groups, what reason do too many companies have for advertising their products as environmentally safe?
    a. It's a way to give the company a better image.
    b. It's a good way to help save the earth.
    c. It makes good market research.
    d. Both a and b.

4. According to Ned Potter, what are consumers being bombarded with?
    a. Cheap, environmentally safe products.
    b. Claims that products are environmentally safe.
    c. Requests for money for environmental causes.
    d. Lies about the products.

INFORMATION MATCH

Watch the next part of the segment. Match each type of product with the environmental claims made on the package or container.

_____ 1. deodorant manufacturers   a. "degradable"
_____ 2. cereal manufacturers   b. "ozone friendly"
_____ 3. trash bag manufacturers   c. "recycled"

LISTENING FOR IMPORTANT INFORMATION

Watch this part of the segment and take notes on the following questions. Then compare your notes with those of another student.

1. Why does Ken Deutsch give supermarket tours?

    _____

    _____

2. What is the Chevron commercial promoting?

_____

_____

3. What is unusual about this type of advertising?

_____

_____

4. According to Michael Picker, what does the evidence show about the Chevron Corporation in California?

_____

_____

5. According to Herbert Chao Gunther, which companies probably do the most green advertising?

_____

_____

6. According to Dan Johnson, why doesn't Chevron use its commercials to explain the facts about what it has done to reduce its hazardous waste?

_____

_____

7. What is the purpose of the task forces that have been established in ten states?

_____

_____

8. According to Joel Makower and many others, what more should be done to control the "green claims" made by companies?

_____

_____

Language Focus

The following sentences are from the video segment. Match the *italicized* words with their equivalents below.

a. improve
b. angry or excited reaction
c. factories where substances are purified

d. be the first to introduce
e. announces officially
f. poisonous

_____ 1. Recently, DuPont announced that its energy unit would *pioneer* the use of new double-hulled oil tankers in order to safeguard the environment.

_____ 2. Consumer groups say too many companies just see the environment as a way to *boost* their image.

_____ 3. That simple message has caused quite a *furor*.

_____ 4. They're just telling everybody what great people they are, and the evidence is that they are major California *toxic* polluters.

_____ 5. Chevron says it has already spent millions to clean up its *refineries*.

_____ 6. I don't really care who *promulgates* the rules.

USEFUL EXPRESSIONS

The sentences below are all spoken on the video. Circle the meaning of the *italicized* expressions.

1. What we hope to do is *make some sense out of* a subject that is confusing to many of us.
   a. develop some feeling for
   b. come to some understanding of
   c. discuss some of the foolishness of

2. Here is a deodorant which says "Ozone friendly, no CFCs or chlorofluorocarbons." *Big deal.* The law doesn't allow them to have CFCs.
   a. So what?
   b. That's really interesting.
   c. That's an important agreement.

3. Really, *when it comes down to it*, the only plastics that are degradable are those plastics that are not made out of an oil-based product.
   a. when the most important factors are considered
   b. when it breaks down or decomposes
   c. when you challenge something in court

4. They promote Chevron's image, saying in effect, "Trust us. *We're on your side* when it comes to the environment."
   a. We're always near you.
   b. We disagree with you.
   c. We support you.

5. I think that we're in desperate need of one set of rules that everyone can live under: *a level playing field.*
   a. a situation that involves more things or people
   b. a situation that is fair to everyone involved
   c. a situation in which there are no rules

6. The risk is that many consumers who want to *do their part* for the environment will give up because they have no basis for deciding what to believe.
   a. work part-time
   b. do only the minimum
   c. assume their responsibility

PHRASAL VERBS

The excerpts below are from the video segment. Complete each sentence by filling in each blank with a phrasal verb from the list. Be sure to change the verb tense if necessary. When you finish, watch the video again and check your answers.

give up   live under   put out   set up   sign up   trip over

Joel Makower: Companies are _____ themselves practically, trying to _____ the newest and the greenest products.

00:42:42-
00:42:49

Ned Potter: Some train seals to applaud themselves, others hire celebrities. _____ for Sprint and they'll donate your money to your favorite cause.

00:43:06-
00:43:14

Ned Potter: Ten states have _____ a task force to make sure green claims are accurate, but many say there should be national guidelines

00:45:49-
00:45:59

either from private groups or the Federal Trade Commission.

00:46:00-
00:46:07
Joel Makower: I don't really care who promulgates the rules, but I think that we're in desperate need of one set of rules that everyone can

_____.

00:46:09-
00:46:20
Ned Potter: The risk is that many consumers who want to do their part for the environment will _____ because if they have no basis for deciding what to believe, they may decide not to believe anything.

COMPARING CULTURES

Discuss the following questions in a small group.

1. Were you surprised or shocked by anything you learned from this video?
2. The video mentioned that US manufacturers pay close attention to market research. In fact, market research showing that Americans want to do business with companies that are concerned about the environment is a major reason that the companies are making environmental claims about their products. What positive and/or negative effects have resulted from such marketing research on consumer concerns about the environment?
3. It has been noted that US companies spend a great deal of money on marketing (including both market research and advertising) and relatively little money on the research and development of products. Based on what you have learned from this video and from what you already know about US business practices, do you think this makes good business sense? Do you think it is ultimately beneficial for the environment? Why or why not?
4. Do businesses in your country focus more on marketing or on research and development? Do you think this makes good business sense? Why or why not?
5. Because Americans are becoming more concerned about the negative effects of manufacturing on the environment, numerous regulations have been passed that make it environmentally safer but economically more difficult for a company to manufacture its products in the United States. To avoid such costly regulations, some U.S. companies have moved their manufacturing operations to countries with fewer or no environmental controls. If you were the head of a manufacturing company, what would you do if new environmental regulations made it more expensive to continue in the U.S. than to move to a country that had no such regulations?

6. Have environmental regulations affected manufacturing companies in your country? If so, how have the companies reacted?

RELATED READING

Read the article *Green Consumerism*, paying attention to what some businesses have been doing to appeal to consumers' concern for a clean environment. Then fill in the chart in the Information Check that follows.

Green Consumerism

Market researchers keeping track of trends in consumer concerns are learning that a clean environment rates high on the list of issues important in Americans' lives. It was even rated higher than a satisfactory sex life by many, according to a Harris Poll finding. What effects does such a trend have on corporate America? A look at some recent environmentally oriented corporate campaigns and decisions reveals that so-called "green" concerns are not taken lightly in today's business world.

Green was seen as more than just a traditional Christmas color when marketing specialists came up with new ways to attract shoppers during the 1990 Christmas season. Several department stores opened the season with special earth-theme boutiques. Bloomingdales' 100% Natural Shops sold products made from recycled materials or all-natural fibers. Also featured were items such as a package containing the ingredients to plant your own tree—soil and a few seeds, as well as the Earth Friendly Bag, which included a canvas shopping bag, foods from a rain forest, and the book *50 Simple Things You Can Do to Save the Earth*. A percentage of the proceeds made from some of the above items was contributed to environmental causes. Similarly, Planet Earth shops were set up in Woodward and Lothrop and John Wanamaker stores in October, 1990. The merchandise sold in these shops was made from recycled materials was designed to save energy. Among the items available were T-shirts carrying earth-oriented messages, stationary made from recycled paper, and energy-conserving products used in winter-proofing your home.

Another corporate decision instigated by consumers' environmental concerns was recently reached by the U.S. record industry. This industry found itself under increasing pressure from CD buyers and even from some artists whose music is sold on CDs to get rid of the most commonly used packaging format, an excessively large, disposable cardboard package called the "long box." Some artists refused to use this packaging, while others designed a more creative version of the long box with the intent that it be kept, rather than thrown away. Consumer activism contributed to the industry's decision to change CD packaging from the larger, paper-wasting long box to a smaller, more environmentally correct form of packaging called the "jewel box." This decision will be effective as of April 1993.

Some department stores and grocery stores have begun to pay attention to the wasteful packaging they send home with the consumer. Check-out bags made of recycled paper or plastic material are increasingly common today. In still other efforts to cut waste, Target Stores, a discount department store in the Midwest, prints its flyers on recyclable paper and has started recycling 75 percent of the store's waste.

These are just a few examples of business response to what has become a highly visible consumer concern. There are sure to be more businesses ready to jump on the bandwagon if the environment continues to be the theme of the '90s.

INFORMATION CHECK

Fill in the chart below with the missing information. The first one has been completed for you.

BUSINESS	GREEN CONSUMERISM
Bloomingdales	*100% Natural Shops sold products made from recycled materials and other "green" items. Some of the profits went to environmental causes.*
Lothrop & John Wanamaker stores	_____ _____ _____
record industry	_____ _____ _____
_____	*Some refused to have their CDs sold in the long box, and others designed creative styles of the long box to be kept, not thrown away.*
department and grocery stores	_____ _____ _____
_____	*prints flyers on recyclable paper; recycles about 75% of store's waste*

FINAL TEAM TASK

The video segment and the reading both told how businesses are trying to appeal to consumers' concerns about the environment. See for yourself what businesses are actually doing to show that they share this concern. Form groups of four to investigate various aspects of this issue.

1. One member in each group should look into one of the following areas:
   A. Advertisements in magazines and newspapers that make "green" claims about a product or corporation
   B. Television advertisements that make "green" claims about a product or corporation
   C. Claims on actual products (usually on the packaging) about the environmental safety of that product. Grocery or hardware stores may be a good place to look.
   D. Retail campaigns or innovations designed to profit from environmental concerns, such as shops or departments with an environmental theme
2. Meet in groups to share the information the members gathered. For each report, discuss the following questions:
   A. What environmental claim is being made?
   B. What market is the claim supposed to appeal to? Example: housewives, students, etc.?
   C. Do you think the claim or campaign will be successful for the business that is marketing the product? That is, will it increase sales?
   D. Do you think the claim or campaign is actually helping to clean up the environment, or at least helping to minimize pollution?

FINAL WRITTEN TASK

OPTION A

Write up a report about the area you investigated for the Final Team Task. Include information your group discussed.

OPTION B

After learning about corporations' false claims to benefit the environment, you feel so angry that you want to voice your opinion. Write a letter to the editor of your local newspaper in which you discuss the problem in general and cite several specific examples. Try to convince the readers that action must be taken to stop the false claims made by businesses.

Segment 5

Beyond 9 to 5

from *20/20*, 3/3/89
Runtime: 15:05
Begin: 46:52

Previewing

KEY QUESTIONS

1. What technological developments in the last decade have radically changed people's lives?
2. How has the concept of a global economy affected the finance industry?
3. Is it necessary for professionals to be in their office 40 hours a week or more to do their job?
4. What are some of the positive and negative effects of technological advances on people's work lives?

DISCUSSION

1. What new electronic devices have you acquired in the past decade?

   _____

   _____

2. Have any of these devices changed your life? If so, in what ways?

   _____

   _____

3. What would your ideal work schedule be?

   _____

   _____

PREDICTIONS

Think about the title *Beyond 9 to 5*. What does it refer to? What information will be included in the video segment? Confirm your predictions after you have watched the entire segment once.

1. Title:

   _____

2. Information:

   a. _____

   b. _____

   c. _____

   d. _____

ESSENTIAL WORDS TO KNOW

The following words are used in the video segment. Familiarize yourself with the meanings of the words. Then in the space that follows write a sentence with the *italicized* word included.

1. *telecommunication*: communication over a distance, such as by telephone, telegraph and fax

   _____

   _____

2. *cellular phone*: telephones that do not have to be in a fixed place to be used; these include car phones, portable phones, etc.

   _____

   _____

3. *laptop computer*: a portable computer that is small enough to carry around and use on your lap

   _____

   _____

4. *modem*: a device used to convert data so that it can be transmitted by telephone and then reconverted to its original form

   _____

   _____

5. *obsolete*: no longer in use

_____

_____

6. *competitive edge*: an advantage over those you are competing against

_____

_____

Global Viewing

CHECKING YOUR COMPREHENSION

First look at the chart below. Then watch the entire segment and check (✔)
the appropriate columns.

00:47:11-
01:01:19

WHO. . .?	ROBERT FRANKLIN	BOB JONES	DONNA KOEHLER
1. can ski in the middle of the day			
2. drives to the office two days a week			
3. has a work day that never ends			
4. has started reading history and the bible			
5. spends three days a week at home and two days in the office			
6. finishes jobs in about half the time it used to take			
7. is interrupted by phone calls when out on dates			
8. has started a horse-raising farm			
9. has experienced a change in sleeping habits			
10. has a more balanced life now			

Intensive Viewing

LISTENING FOR DETAILS

00:47:25-
00:49:01

Watch this part of the segment and choose the best answer to each question.

1. According to Hugh Downs, which four forms of telecommunication have caused a revolution in how and when people work?
   a. Satellites, modems, fax machines, and cellular phones.
   b. Computers, satellites, fax machines, and cellular phones.
   c. Computers, modems, fax machines, and cellular phones.
   d. Computers, modems, satellites, and cellular phones.

2. According to Bob Brown, which type of business or industry was the among the first to be affected by the telecommunications revolution?
   a. The advertising business.
   b. The construction industry.
   c. The travel industry.
   d. The financial markets.

3. What change in the financial markets is NOT mentioned in the video?
   a. The shift toward global trends.
   b. Hyperactive computer transactions.
   c. Increasing numbers of women in the business.
   d. The trend toward making 9-5 jobs obsolete.

4. How many cellular phones were in use the year before the video was produced?
   a. Almost none.
   b. Almost one million.
   c. More than 1.7 million.
   d. More than 17 million.

LISTENING FOR IMPORTANT INFORMATION

00:49:02-
00:57:45

Watch the next part of the segment and take brief notes on the answers to the following questions. Then compare your notes with those of another student. If you disagree, watch the segment again.

1. Why are communications gadgets important to Robert Franklin?

   _____

   _____

2. What problem does Robert Franklin have because of his work?

_____

_____

3. On the night that the ABC news team stayed with Robert Franklin, what four places did he get telephone calls from?

_____

_____

4. When does Robert Franklin's work week begin and when does it end?

_____

_____

5. In what three ways is Bob Jones's life different from Robert Franklin's?

   a. _____

   b. _____

   c. _____

6. What two electronic devices have made it possible for people in all kinds of businesses to work away from their offices?

_____

_____

7. How do power company employees in Sweden make use of telecommunications devices?

_____

_____

8. According to Alvin Toffler, in what sense are people becoming liberated?

_____

_____

TRUE OR FALSE?

00:55:10-
00:56:25

Read the sentences below. Then watch the next part of the segment and decide if they are true or false. Write *T* or *F*.

_____ 1. Donna Koehler used to spend five days a week at her office.

_____ 2. It takes her an hour to commute between her home and her office.

_____ 3. She now goes into the office three days a week.

_____ 4. She works as a financial analyst.

_____ 5. She uses a computer to send the work she does at home to her office.

_____ 6. She feels she is more productive working at home.

INFORMATION MATCH

00:57:08-
00:58:04

Watch this part of the segment and match the people with their views about management and telecommuting.

a. Donna Koehler   b. Alvin Toffler   c. Heidi Toffler

_____ 1. Management is used to using time at the desk as a measure of productivity and performance.

_____ 2. Managers from the old days still think people won't work unless somebody is looking over their shoulder.

_____ 3. We're going to need millions of employees who are self-starters.

_____ 4. We're going to need employees who come up with new ideas.

_____ 5. We need managements that are not afraid of new ideas.

_____ 6. Telecommuting forces managers to begin to evaluate employees based on the product that those employees produce.

LISTENING CLOZE

00:58:07-
00:59:14

Watch the next part of the video and fill in the blanks with the missing words. Then compare your answers with those of another student.

Bob Brown: But the same technology that has _____ _____ the life of Donna Koehler has been, as we've seen, _____ to currency trader Robert Franklin, who can't escape it even on a squash _____. So another of the big questions we'll be _____ is, how do you control it without letting it control you?

Dr. Meyer Friedman: I think a cellular telephone sometimes can be _____ , but if you want to do too many things in too little time, then you're _____ _____.

Bob Brown: One of the leading experts on _____ _____ and heart care in this country is Dr. Meyer Friedman of San Francisco.

Dr. Meyer Friedman: We have another man that's trying to use his cellular telephone and at the same time _____. Well, he puts his _____ into the cigarette lighter place, but you know, then he can't drive and so he's _____ himself. I think you know you're in trouble when you cannot sit and listen to music, let's say, and not _____ _____. Or that you can watch little children play and not feel you're _____ _____.

Language Focus

TELECOMMUNICATIONS AND THE TELEPHONE

Using the telephone is such a common part of everyday life that we usually take it for granted. But when you have to talk on the phone in English and English is not your native language, it may not be such an easy task. How familiar are you with the phrases that are commonly used when talking on the phone? Check (✔) the response that is most appropriate in each of the following situations.

1. Calling Directory Assistance
   A: Directory Assistance.
   B: a. _____ I'd like the number for John Adler, please.
   　 b. _____ Please give me John Adler's number.
   　 c. _____ I need John Adler's number, please.

2. Making a collect call
   A: Operator.
   B: a. _____ I'd like to talk to John, and I'd like him to pay for this call.
   　 b. _____ This is Niki and I'd like to charge this call to John.
   　 c. _____ I'd like to make a collect call from Niki to John.

3. Responding to someone who has dialed the wrong number
   A: Hello.
   B: May I speak to Tim, please?
   A: a. _____ I'm sorry. He's not here.
   　 b. _____ He doesn't have this phone number. I'm sorry.
   　 c. _____ I'm sorry. You must have the wrong number.

4. Responding to a formal call
   A: A & S Communications.
   B: I'd like to speak to Sarah Wirth, please.
   A: a. _____ Who are you?
      b. _____ May I tell her who's calling?
      c. _____ What would you like to speak to her about?

5. Indicating that someone is not at home
   A: Hello.
   B: May I speak to Ann, please?
   A: a. _____ She's not here right now. May I take a message?
      b. _____ She's not at home. Can I help you?
      c. _____ She's not here. Please call again.

6. Identifying yourself to a caller
   A: Hello.
   B: Hello. May I speak to Kim, please?
   A: a. _____ My name is Kim.
      b. _____ I'm Kim.
      c. _____ This is Kim.

LEAVING A MESSAGE ON AN ANSWERING MACHINE

Here are a few tips for leaving a message on an answering machine:

- Speak clearly.
- Leave your name.
- Indicate the time and day of your call.
- State the reason you are calling.
- Leave a phone number where you can be reached.

Work in pairs. In this exercise, you and your partner will practice leaving messages on an answering machine. Your messages should fit the following situation:

Two friends (A and B) have made tentative plans to go to a movie together. A leaves a message on B's answering machine, suggesting a time and a place to meet. B gets A's message and then leaves a message on A's machine, indicating whether he or she can meet A at the time and place suggested.

After deciding who will be A and who will be B, follow this procedure for recording and evaluating your messages:

1. A records his/her message on a cassette recorder.
2. B plays back A's message and evaluates it, using Form A on page 57.
3. Then B records a message in response to A's message.
4. A plays back B's message and evaluates it, using Form B on page 57.

```
┌──────────────────────────────────────────────────────────────────────┐
│                            FORM A                                       │
│  Did the caller . . .                                  Yes      No      │
│  1. speak clearly?                                      ❑        ❑       │
│  2. leave his/her name?                                 ❑        ❑       │
│  3. say what time and day it is?                        ❑        ❑       │
│  4. say where to meet?                                  ❑        ❑       │
│  5. say when to call back?                              ❑        ❑       │
│  6. ask B to call back?                                 ❑        ❑       │
│  7. leave the number where he/she can be reached?       ❑        ❑       │
└──────────────────────────────────────────────────────────────────────┘

┌──────────────────────────────────────────────────────────────────────┐
│                            FORM B                                       │
│  Did the caller . . .                                  Yes      No      │
│  1. speak clearly?                                      ❑        ❑       │
│  2. leave his/her name?                                 ❑        ❑       │
│  3. say what time and day it is?                        ❑        ❑       │
│  4. say if he/she could meet A?                         ❑        ❑       │
│  5. leave the number where he/she could be reached?*    ❑        ❑       │
│                                                                         │
│  * Only necessary if B is at a number different from the usual one and  │
│  wants A to call back.                                                  │
└──────────────────────────────────────────────────────────────────────┘
```

Postviewing

COMPARING CULTURES

Discuss the following questions in small groups.

1. Were you surprised or shocked by anything you learned from this video?

2. Are the social and lifestyle changes that have come about because of technological advances positive or negative? Explain your answer.

3. Because telecommunication devices make possible the instant worldwide transmission of information, do you think that the differences between cultures will decrease? Give some examples to support your opinion.

4. Did the video show any lifestyle changes due to telecommunications that could never occur in your culture? If so, give specific examples.

5. Do you feel at all threatened by any of the technological changes shown in the video? If so, explain further.

6. Do you think that your parents' generation feels threatened by any of the technological changes shown in the video? Explain your answer.

RELATED READING

Read the article *Is Technology Getting Out of Hand?* to answer the questions that follow.

Is Technology Getting Out of Hand?

"We're not home right now. Please leave a message after the beep."

Remember the first time you heard the beep after the recorded message? If you're like many people, your palms got sweaty, you became instantly tongue-tied, your mind went blank. Then you hung up the phone. Today, after more than a decade of conditioning, you respond automatically to that beep. You may even have become so conditioned that after dialing a number and hearing a succession of rings, the absence of an answering machine arouses frustration and anger. There are even times, perhaps, when you wait to make certain phone calls until you are sure that you will reach a machine instead of having to face an unpleasant human interaction. In fact, fairly involved conversations can be carried out today without ever having live voice contact between interlocutors by playing what is often referred to as "telephone tag".

New technology often causes much fear and resistance when it debuts. Some people are afraid that anything electronic and programmable is too complicated for them to learn how to use. Take programming the VCR as an example. For anyone born after 1970, this is probably second nature. But ask their parents to perform this task, and it's a different story. Another fear is that the explosive increase in automated devices may have a dehumanizing effect on our lives. Chores that used to involve at least one face-to-face encounter, like depositing or withdrawing money from the bank are now routinely done at any hour of the day or night by pressing a few buttons at the nearest ATM. The fear can reach almost phobic proportions when one considers the proliferation of new services such as home shopping and dial-a -movie, which are transacted within one's living room.

Before you let yourself imagine a science fiction world where each person lives in an individual cubicle fed by a vast network of cables carrying incoming and outgoing electronic signals, remember that the same fear and resistance were undoubtedly caused by the introduction of technologically intimidating and dehumanizing devices as the telephone and television.

COMPREHENSION QUESTIONS

1. In the second paragraph, what does the word *tongue-tied* mean?

_____

_____

2. What is meant by the phrase *your mind went blank* in the second paragraph?

_____

_____

3. What is "telephone tag," described in the second paragraph?

_____

_____

4. What are the two fears people have about new technology?

_____

_____

5. What chores used to be done by contacting people face-to-face that are now done by interacting with a machine?

_____

_____

6. Does the author think that people should be frightened by new technology? Refer to statements in the reading to support your answer.

_____

_____

DISCUSSION QUESTIONS

1. How did you react to telephone answering machines when they first came out? How do you feel about using them now?
2. What other new devices in addition to those mentioned might be feared because they could have a "dehumanizing" effect on our lives?
3. This reading mentions new technology that makes our home life easier. What new technology has changed your educational or work experience? How has it changed your experience?
4. Which of the new devices mentioned in the reading exist in your country?
5. Does your country have other, more–advanced telecommunications devices that do not exist in the United States?

FINAL TEAM TASK: DESIGNING THE FUTURE

The class as a whole is a company that designs new products for home use, education, and the workplace. Planning has begun for the release of a new line of products: Products for the Year 2000. In groups of 3 to 5 members, you will act as design teams for this company.

1. Each team must design three new products: one for use in the home, one for educational purposes, and one for use at work.
2. Each team must present its three new products at a meeting of the entire company. Your product presentation should include at least a detailed description of each product and how it will benefit our lives. Pictures of your team's products are also acceptable.
3. Of all the products presented, the company (class) as a whole must choose three products, one from each category (home, education, work), to display at a product convention.

FINAL WRITTEN TASK

Imagine you live in the year 2020. What will your daily routine be like? How will technology have changed your domestic life? Your job? Will you have to go to an office to work? Write an essay in which you describe an average day in your life in the year 2020. Be as realistic or as fantastic as you want.

Segment 6

The Joys and Risks of the "Daddy Track"

from *Nightline*, 8/14/91
Runtime: 8:30
Begin: 1:01:41

Previewing

KEY QUESTIONS

1. Why do men today want to be more involved in raising their children than did men of their fathers' generation?
2. What benefits do some American companies offer to men who want to spend more time with their families?
3. Why do few men take advantage of these benefits?
4. How does becoming a father affect the careers of some American men?

DISCUSSION

1. How involved was your father in raising you and your siblings (brothers and sisters)?

_____

_____

2. (for the males) If you had children, would you want to spend more or less time with your children than your father did? Explain your answer.

_____

_____

3. (for the females) If you had children, would you want your husband to spend more or less time with your children than your father did? Explain your answer.

_____

_____

4. (for the males) Would you be willing to slow down your career so that you could be more involved in raising your children? Why or why not?

_____

_____

5. (for the females) Would you want your husband to slow down his career so that he could be more involved in raising your children? Why or why not?

_____

_____

PREDICTION

Work in groups. Based on the title of the segment, *The Joys and Risks of the "Daddy Track,"* the discussion you've had with your classmates, and your own background knowledge, what do you think you will see and hear on the video? Write down four items under each of the headings below. Confirm your predictions after you have watched the entire segment once.

SIGHTS (THINGS YOU EXPECT TO SEE)	WORDS (WORDS YOU EXPECT TO HEAR)
1. _____	_____
2. _____	_____
3. _____	_____
4. _____	_____

ESSENTIAL WORDS TO KNOW

The *italicized* words in the sentences below are used in the video. Read the sentences and suggest your own definition for each word or phrase.

1. Senior executives are at the top of the *corporate ladder*.

    corporate ladder: _____

2. The personnel director announced that the company would soon be introducing a policy of *flexible hours* for its employees.

    flexible hours: _____

3. The company offers five days of *paternity leave* to new fathers.

    paternity leave: _____

4. The female employees complained that the company's policies *discriminated* against women.

    discriminate (v): _____

5. They are *suing* the company for the money that it owes them.

    sue (v): _____

6. Some working parents leave their children in *day care centers* while they are at work.

    day care center: _____

Global Viewing

GETTING THE MAIN IDEAS

Read the following sentences. Then watch the video again and decide whether each sentence is true or false. Write *T* or *F*.

01:02:35-
01:08:20

_____ 1. The revolution for women in American society has had little effect on men.

_____ 2. Surveys show that many men would like to trade a slower career path for more time with their families.

_____ 3. Many men in the United States take paternity leave in order to spend more time with their children.

_____ 4. In the majority of American families, both parents are working.

_____ 5. Many American men experience a conflict between work and family responsibilities.

_____ 6. Most big and medium-sized companies in the United States offer paternity leave.

Intensive Viewing

LISTENING CLOZE

01:02:35-
01:03:18

Watch this part of the segment and fill in the blanks with the missing words. Then compare your answers with those of another student.

Chris Wallace: It should be no surprise, but it's turning out that the revolution for women in our society has also become a revolution for men. As more and more women go into the _____ , men are having to pick up some of the slack at home. As women try to balance the _____ of family and career, men are finding they must do the same thing. And, as with the women's revolution, it isn't _____. Surveys find that by _____ margins, men would be willing to trade a slower _____ _____ for more family time. At least, that's what they say. But when you talk to personnel directors of companies offering _____ _____ or _____ _____ , they say _____ men take advantage of these benefits. They're _____ of losing their place on the _____ _____.

LISTENING FOR DETAILS

01:03:30-
01:08:02

Watch this part of the segment and choose the best answer to each of the questions.

1. What men are part of "the new fatherhood"?
   a. Men who want to be involved with their children.
   b. Men who have to be involved with their children.
   c. Men who have little interest in being involved with their children.
   d. Both a and b.

2. In how many American families do both parents work?
   a. One out of two.
   b. One out of three.
   c. Two out of three.
   d. Three out of five.

3. When John Graykowsky interviewed for jobs at law firms, what did he do that was unusual?
   a. He took his children along on the interviews.
   b. He asked for the interviews to take place at his home.
   c. He set down certain conditions regarding travel and work time.
   d. Both a and b.

4. Why are John Graykowsky and John Canise called "the lucky ones"?
   a. They have part-time jobs.
   b. They don't take any work home.
   c. Their companies have day care centers where they can leave their children while they are at work.
   d. The time they spend with their children doesn't cause them trouble at work.

5. Which of the following is NOT true about Jeff Coulter?
   a. He was fired from his job at Microsoft.
   b. He says he worked no more than 50 hours per week.
   c. He tried to get home from work before his children went to bed.
   d. Both a and b.

6. Which of the following was NOT said or suggested by Leanne Boyle?
   a. That Microsoft hires people who "kill" themselves with work.
   b. That the survivors at Microsoft are not married.
   c. That it's a disadvantage to have any priority other than work.
   d. That a lot of people at Microsoft are spending time with their families.

7. What claim or claims is Jeff Coulter making in his legal suit against Microsoft?
   a. That he was discriminated against because of his marital status.
   b. That Microsoft has a legal obligation to offer day care for its employees' children.
   c. That his boss secretly recorded her conversations with him.
   d. Both a and b.

8. What percentage of American men surveyed said they would accept a slower career path in exchange for more family time?
   a. 50 percent.
   b. 60 percent.
   c. 70 percent.
   d. 80 percent.

9. According to Gwen Weld of Microsoft, why was Jeff Coulter fired from his job?
   a. He was not successful in overall account management.
   b. He was not successful in managing his employees.
   c. He was spending too much time with his children.
   d. Both a and b.

10. Which of the following statements is NOT true?
   a. Many American men are discouraged from believing it is possible to be successful at a fast–track job and also be a family man.
   b. James Levine believes that some men try to hide the conflict they feel between work and family.
   c. Steven Shorkey's company doesn't have a paternity leave policy.
   d. Steven Shorkey took time off from work when his first child was born.

Language Focus

USING AND UNDERSTANDING IDIOMS

Complete each sentence below with the correct idiom. Then compare your answers with those of another student and discuss the meaning of each idiom.

wasn't cutting it	have a hand in	summed it up
pick up some of the slack	took advantage of	

1. As more and more women go into the workplace, men find they have to _____ at home.

2. Jeff Coulter's boss said, "You're at a company where it's a disadvantage to be married." Jeff thought that this _____ concerning his company's reason for firing him.

3. Microsoft said that the reason Jeff was fired was not that he was a family man, but that he just _____.

4. Steven Shorkey was lucky that his company offered paternity leave, and he _____ this policy.

5. In the United States today, the economic reality is that both working parents _____ raising their children.

SPEAKING INFORMALLY: FILLERS

When people speak in an unplanned, informal way, they often use *fillers* — short phrases such as *you know* or *I mean* that don't really add anything to the meaning of the sentence and would not normally be used in planned or formal speech. Listen to the following excerpts from the video and fill in the blanks with the fillers you hear.

1. *John Graykowsky:* It's your child, and it makes you think of your children first in the morning and last at night, and you _____ build in your work in between.

   01:04:05-
   01:04:15

2. *Jeff Coulter:* My manager clearly told me, _____ , "You're at a company where it's a disadvantage to be married." _____ , that pretty much summed it up.

   01:04:43-
   01:04:49

3. *Jeff Coulter:* It was really a perception of time. I got in early, and I was typically the first or the second one in the office. And not everybody's around to see you when you come in early, but they're all there to see you when you leave, _____ , at 5:00 or 5:30, whatever.

   01:05:06-
   01:05:16

4. *Leanne Boyle:* Microsoft hires everybody who's killing themselves. So everybody who's killing themselves is competing against other people who are killing themselves and it's, _____ ,survival of the fittest.

   01:05:24-
   01:05:27

FIELDWORK

Observe some native speakers conversing informally in English. You may make your observations by watching a television show or video, or by listening to "live" conversations. What fillers do the speakers use? In what situations do they use them? Use the chart below to list the fillers you hear and the situations in which they are used. After you have finished, compare and discuss your findings in small groups. Then report your group's conclusions to the class.

FILLERS	SITUATIONS
Example: *you know*	*two friends talking at a bus stop*

Postviewing

COMPARING CULTURES

Discuss the following questions in small groups.

1. Were you surprised or shocked by anything on the video? If so, what?
2. In what ways, if any, are the fathers in the video similar to fathers in your own culture?
3. In what ways, if any, are they different?
4. In two out of three U.S. families, both parents are working. To the best of your knowledge, how does this compare with the situation in your own country?
5. Some U.S. companies offer benefits such as parental leave or flexible hours to employees who want to spend time with their families. What type of benefits do companies in your country offer?
6. Jeff Coulter is suing Microsoft, making the claim that he was discriminated against because of his marital status. Do people (either male or female) in your country ever sue their employers on the basis of such discrimination? Why or why not?

RELATED READING: THE DADDY TRACK

Read the article *The Emergence of the Daddy Track* and answer the comprehension and opinion questions that follow.

The Emergence of the Daddy Track

Hollywood has always shown us a reflection of the lifestyle trends of the day. Those of us born in the '50s remember the idyllic families we watched on *Leave It to Beaver* and *The Donna Reed Show*. In those days the mother was usually seen in the kitchen wearing an apron. The father came home from work, briefcase in hand, to a hot-cooked meal prepared by his waiting wife. Then the whole family sat down at the dinner table and the comedy began, often with the wife informing her husband of some trouble one of the children had gotten into. This was the cue for the father to step in as disciplinarian, and that was usually the extent of the father's input in child-rearing matters.

As women began to enter the workforce in large numbers and the perfect nuclear family faded from the picture, a new Hollywood dad appeared on the screen. In *Kramer versus Kramer* Dustin Hoffman as Ted Kramer found himself suddenly without a wife and in sole custody of a five–year–old child. Hilarious scenes in the kitchen with father and son making French toast showed how inept Ted Kramer was at any family duties other than bringing home the bacon. Out of necessity, he learned and took on all the duties of raising a child, much to his boss's disapproval. Fearing that Ted would not be able to stay on the fast track with his new family commitments, he warned Ted, "I got to count on you for 110 percent, 7 days a week, 24 hours a day. I can't be concerned about you worrying about a kid with a runny nose." This was 1979, about a decade before the idea of the "daddy track" surfaced.

Today, companies are beginning to realize that with more than half of the women of child-bearing age working full time, men are going to be assuming some of the family responsibilities at home. Although bosses like the fictional character in *Kramer versus Kramer* are still around in real corporate life, companies are adapting to this change in various ways. Some, like DuPont, offer part-time hours to all men and women employees, so that they can spend more time at home. One couple at DuPont, both engineers, share their time off and job: Tom stays home with the baby for a week while Mary goes in to work, and Mary stays home the next week while Tom goes to work. Some companies offer flexible work hours so that parents can work around their childrens' school or day care schedules. Another sign of change is the growing number of firms offering paternity leave. The Bureau of Labor Statistics found that 17 percent of medium and large companies offered men some form of parental leave in 1988; in 1989 that number had risen to 20 percent.

With flexible hours and paternity leave still relatively new, the effects of such policies on careers and business are not really known. A spokeswoman for DuPont, Faith Wohl, says that her company wants to employ "balanced people. . . . We're not looking for people who are going to cloister themselves in the corporation 18 hours a day and lose track of the outside world." Yet Lester Korn, an executive recruiter, believes that the competitive nature of the corporate world does not really provide for the "daddy track". He warns, "If you decide that you want to spend time with your children, you are going to lose your place in your peer group, and you're going to hurt your career if you spend a fair amount of time doing this."

COMPREHENSION QUESTIONS

1. What does the phrase "bringing home the bacon" mean in the context "Hilarious scenes in the kitchen with father and son making French toast showed how inept Ted Kramer was at any family duties other than bringing home the bacon"?

   _____

   _____

2. When did the concept of the "daddy track" come about?

   _____

   _____

3. What three things are some U.S. companies doing to make it easier for male or female employees to spend more time at home?

a. _____

b. _____

c. _____

IN YOUR OPINION

1. According to Faith Wohl, DuPont wants to employ "balanced people" who don't spend 18 hours a day on the job. Do you think this practice makes good business sense? Why or why not?

_____

_____

2. Based on the information in the article, do you think the number of U.S. companies offering benefits such as flexible hours and paternity leave will decrease, stay the same, or continue to grow? Give reasons for your answer.

_____

_____

3. According to the article, the effects on careers and business of such new policies as flexible hours and paternity leave are not really known. What do you think might be some possible effects, both positive and negative, of such policies on careers and business?

_____

_____

RELATED READING: THE FAMILY-LEAVE BILL

Read the article *The Family-Leave Bill* and discuss the questions that follow.

The Family-Leave Bill

The days when companies ask that men taking paternity leave call it "vacation days" may now be over. On Friday, February 5, 1993, President Clinton signed the Family-Leave Bill. This bill requires that companies that employ a minimum of 50 people must offer 12 weeks of unpaid leave a year to any employee needing to take care of a newborn or adopted infant or a sick family member. Although employees taking advantage of family leave are not paid during this period, their job is guaranteed and their health insurance coverage is continued. The signing of this bill makes the United States one of the last industrialized nations to offer some guarantee that a woman be allowed time off after giving birth. It goes further than regulations in certain other countries that have similar laws for women but not for men.

GROUP DISCUSSION QUESTIONS

1. Do you think this bill will have a big impact on the number of men who decide to accept the "daddy track"? Why or why not?
2. Does your country have a law similar to the new bill concerning family leave passed in the United States? In what ways does it differ?

FINAL TEAM TASK

OPTION A: CONDUCTING A SURVEY

To find out more about men's attitudes toward work and family obligations and their companies' adjustments to men's changing role in the family, you will conduct a survey.

1. Work in groups of 3 to 5 and make up a questionnaire. Include at least five yes/no questions to ask men about their attitudes toward work and family obligations and their companies' adjustments to men's changing role in the family. For example: "Would you like to be more involved in raising your children?" or "Does your company offer flexible hours to employees who want to spend more time at home?"
2. Use your questionnaire to interview a cross-section of men who are employed in different kinds of jobs. When you take the survey, count the yes and no responses to each question. Take notes on any interesting comments that people make.
3. When your group meets again, summarize the information you have gathered and prepare an oral report to present to the class.

Option B: Presenting a Skit

Work in small groups and make up a skit using the "daddy track" as a theme. Your skit can be either a comedy or a drama.

1. To get started, brainstorm possible situations. For example, a serious business meeting in which several men get off the topic and steer the discussion toward baby feeding schedules, or a family discussion involving a couple who share work and time off schedules that cause a lot of confusion.
2. Write out the script.
3. Rehearse the skit.
4. Present the skit to the class.

FINAL WRITTEN TASK

Option A

If you chose Option A as your final team task, write a two-paragraph summary of the survey you conducted. In the first paragraph, provide an introduction, telling what the survey was about and giving a general description of the men who were included in the survey. Do NOT give specific information such as the names of the men who were interviewed. In the second paragraph, summarize and interpret the results of the survey.

Option B

Write your reaction (one-page maximum) agreeing or disagreeing with the statement below.

Any man who takes time off from his job or goes on paternal leave in order to spend more time at home with his family isn't really very serious about his career.

Segment 7

Bilingual Education

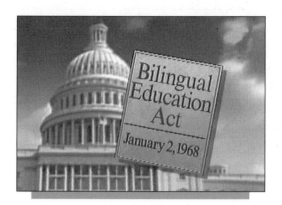

from World News Tonight, 7/4-7/5/89
Runtime: 10:34
Begin: 1:08:32

Previewing

KEY QUESTIONS

1. Do immigrant children in U.S. schools learn English more rapidly if they are put in classes taught only in English?
2. What problems can arise for immigrant children who learn academic subjects in a second language?
3. Should children whose native language is not English be initially taught in bilingual programs that emphasize their native language?
4. How long should children be kept in bilingual programs before entering classes taught completely in English?

DISCUSSION

1. Does your country have a declared official language? If so, does this fact have any legal effect on education, advertising, signs in public places, or other aspects of life?

_____

_____

2. Are there bilingual programs in your country? If so, who attends schools with these programs?

_____

_____

3. If you were to have children in the U.S., would you want your children to begin school attending classes taught for the most part in English or classes taught in both your native language and in English? Why?

_____

_____

PREDICTIONS

The video segment debates whether children who don't speak English should be sent to bilingual classes or to classes taught in English. Make predictions about what reasons each side will give to support their side of the debate. Confirm your predictions after you have watched the entire segment once.

FOR BILINGUAL CLASSES

Reason:_____

Reason:_____

Reason:_____

FOR CLASSES TAUGHT MOSTLY IN ENGLISH

Reason:_____

Reason:_____

Reason:_____

ESSENTIAL WORDS TO KNOW

The *italicized* words and phrases in each of the following sentences are used in the video. Read the sentences and suggest your own definition for each word or phrase.

1. We hope there will be peaceful *transition* from the old system of goverment to the new.

    *transition:*_____

2. The children were studying in a special education program before they started studying in *mainstream* classes.

    mainstream: _____

3. He was so *immersed* in his work that he didn't notice me.

    immerse: _____

4. She is *committing* all her money to the project.

    *commit (v):*_____

5. The Germans and the Italians *endorsed* the plan, but the French government refused to support it.

    endorse (v): _____

6. A number of methods for teaching languages claim to be based on *linguistic* theory.

    linguistic: _____

Global Viewing

INFORMATION MATCH
What kind of educational program does each of the following people support? Watch the entire segment and check the appropriate column.

01:08:45-
01:17:47

PERSON	BILINGUAL PROGRAMS	CLASSES TAUGHT MOSTLY IN ENGLISH
Kathryn Bricker		
James Crawford		
James Lyons		
Maria Ott		

Intensive Viewing

LISTENING FOR DETAILS
Watch this part of the segment and choose the best answer to each question.

01:08:45-
01:11:40

1. How many immigrants enter the United States each year?
    a. Less than half a million
    b. More than half a million.
    c. More than a million.
    d. More than a million and a half.

2. What is the focus of the debate about bilingual education?
    a. Whether or not immigrant children need to learn English.
    b. Who should teach English to teach immigrant children.?
    c. Whether or not immigrant chiildren should receive any instruction in their native language.
    d. Whether or not immigrant children should receive instruction in academic subjects other than English.

3. Which of the following is NOT a feature of typical bilingual education programs?
    a. The children start out taking 45 minutes of English a day.
    b. From the beginning, the children are taught most of their academic subjects in English.
    c. The amount of English instruction increases.
    d. The children change to all–English classes by the third grade.

4. Which of the following is NOT true about Kathryn Bricker?
    a. She is head of an organization called U.S. English.
    b. She believes that children should be taught in all-English classes from the beginning.
    c. She believes that native language instruction helps children learn English faster.
    d. Both a and b.

5. Which of the following is true about James Crawford?
    a. He has studied the history of bilingual education.
    b. He believes that bilingual education programs are doing a good job.
    c. He believes that English-only programs help children learn English.
    d. Both a and b.

PUTTING EVENTS IN ORDER

01:12:08-
01:12:45

Read the sentences below, which describe events in the history of bilingual education in the United States. Then watch the part of the video segment in which Ron Claiborne summarizes these events. As you watch, put the events in the correct order by numbering them from 1 to 7. The first event has been numbered for you.

_____	A new tide of Asian and Hispanic immigration began.
_____	World War I broke out.
1	Bilingual education was common in the U.S.
_____	Americans turned against bilingualism for the first time.
_____	Many immigrants from southern and eastern Europe arrived in the United States.
_____	The U.S. Congress passed the Bilingual Education Act.
_____	The civil rights movement began in the United States.

TRUE OR FALSE?

Read the following sentences. Then watch this part of the segment and decide whether each sentence is true or false. Write *T* or *F*.

01:13:00-
01:13:38

_____ 1. Two major government studies of bilingual education supported native-language teaching methods.

_____ 2. The Reagan and Bush administrations were strongly influenced by these reports.

_____ 3. The Reagan and Bush administrations increased funding for programs based largely on native–language instruction.

_____ 4. Policymakers today focus on teaching English to children as quickly as possible.

_____ 5. The most innovative and successful bilingual education programs lean toward more native–language instruction.

LISTENING CLOZE

Watch this part of the segment and fill in the blanks with the missing words. Then compare your answers with those of another student.

01:13:44-
01:14:32

Peter Jennings: Tonight we put the subject of bilingual education back on the American Agenda. Last night, in examining the _____ over bilingual education in America, we noted the growing trend towards forcing _____ students to learn English as _____ as possible, which of course means _____ them to give up their native language quickly as well. Tonight Ron Claiborne reports on two schools that use a different _____ and where students seem to do much _____ .

Ron Claiborne: At San Fernando Elementary School in Los Angeles County, the overwhelming _____ of students start school speaking only _____ . But instead of trying to get these children into all-English class in just a few _____ , this school takes an _____ approach.

NOTETAKING

First look over the outline on page 78. Then watch this part of the segment and complete the outline with the important information.

01:14:40-
01:17:30

I. Eastman Project
   A. Similarities to traditional bilingual education programs:
      1. _____

      2. _____

   B. Differences from traditional bilingual education programs:
      1. _____

      2. _____

   C. Theory the project is based on:

      _____

      _____

   D. Results of the project:

      _____

      _____

II. Two-Way Bilingual Education Program
   A. Differences from traditional bilingual education programs:
      1. _____

      2. _____

   B. Results of the program:

      _____

      _____

Language Focus

VOCABULARY CHECK

The following excerpts are from the video segment. Match the *italicized* words with their definitions below.

a. related to ideas formed in the mind   d. strange or unexpected element
b. untrue belief or explanation   e. strong feeling
c. increasing

_____ 1. We have been *accumulating* evidence that bilingual programs are doing a good job.
_____ 2. Actually, that's more *myth* than fact.

      _____ 3. Then a flood of immigrants from southern and eastern Europe, along with anti-German war *fervor*, turned Americans against bilingualism.

      _____ 4. The *irony* is that this is happening at a time when the most innovative and successful bilingual education projects are going in the opposite direction.

      _____ 5. The Eastman Project is based on current linguistic *theory* that children learn best if they first develop thinking and conceptual skills in their primary language.

MAKING COMPARISONS AND CONTRASTS

Several bilingual education programs were discussed in this segment. In comparing these programs, the reporter used words that commonly express comparisons and contrasts. Listen to the two comparisons given in the video segment and fill in the blanks with the words you hear that show similarity or difference.

Ron Claiborne: At this school, children use their native language for most of their classwork. It's called the Eastman Project. The children do study English, just ____ in traditional bilingual education programs. But _____ those programs, there is no pressure to transfer into all-English classes by third grade. _____ , the transition may not occur until fifth or even sixth grade. And while the children learn English, they study academic subjects in the language in which they're comfortable.

01:14:40-
01:15:26

Maria Ott: What's _____ is the emphasis. They have a solid academic foundation in Spanish before they move over into an all-English program of instruction.

Ron Claiborne: At Spreckels Elementary School in San Diego, they _____ use prolonged native language study. _____ here, there's a _____ . At this school, while Spanish-speaking children study English, English speakers study Spanish. It's called Two-way Bilingual Education, each group of children learning the other's language. By sixth grade, all students take most classes in English, _____ they also continue with Spanish. The two-way program at Spreckels has been effective not just at teaching languages to _____ groups but also in

01:16:25-
01:17:22

teaching academic subjects. Both English– and Spanish–speaking kids do _____ on achievement tests _____ their counterparts in other San Diego public schools.

Now list the comparison/contrast words you heard. Also add to the list any other terms you know which are used to compare and contrast items.

SIMILAR	DIFFERENT
_____	_____
_____	_____
_____	_____
_____	_____
_____	_____

PRACTICE MAKING COMPARISONS AND CONTRASTS

Think about the English classes you took in junior or senior high school. Now think about the English classes you are taking now. Are they taught in the same way? Do you do similar activities? Do you practice the same skills? What aspects of your English classes then are similar to or different from the classes you are taking now?

1. Use words from the list above to come up with at least three similarities and three differences in your English studies then and now.
2. Discuss these similarities and differences with a partner, using some of the words you heard used in the video segment in making your comparison.
3. Be prepared to give a short oral summary to the class in which you compare your English classes then and now.

Postviewing

COMPARING CULTURES

Discuss the following questions in small groups.

1. Were you surprised or shocked by anything you learned from this video?
2. Even though almost all U.S. citizens have ancestors who originally immigrated to the United States without speaking English, many citizens have very negative feelings toward the latest immigrants who don't yet speak English. Why do you think this is so?

3. Do many people in your country have negative feelings toward immigrants who don't speak the native language of your country? If so, discuss their reactions to newly arrived immigrants.
4. Some people in the United States, like those in the U.S. English movement, believe in the idea of the United States as a melting pot where people of many different ethnic origins blend together to create one culture. Yet one can find many subcultures, each with its own particular ethnic characteristics, within the country. What is the ethnic blend in your own country like? Is there one main ethnic group or several diverse ethnic subcultures? What is the feeling toward ethnic subcultures in your country?
5. Now that you have heard about the strengths and weaknesses of bilingual and mainstream type education programs, what kind of program would you send your child to if you were going to raise a family in the U.S.? What are the reasons for your choice?

RELATED READING

Read the article *Does the U.S. Need an Official Language?* and answer the questions that follow.

Does the U.S. Need an Official Language?

In a California hospital with a high percentage of Filipino nurses (and patients), the staff was forbidden to speak any language other than English while at work, including the time they were on breaks. Several largely Asian Los Angeles suburbs have passed city laws that restrict the posting of non-English signs. Some homeless shelters have even barred those who don't speak English from entering. Incidents such as these illustrate the climate in which a movement to make English the official language of the United States is gaining strength.

By 1990 more than 15 states had passed laws designating English as their official language. The organized force behind this movement is a group called U.S. English. One of the founding members of this movement, S.I. Hayakawa, fearing that the U.S. had begun to foster "a policy of 'bilingualism,'" believed that English would soon be competing with other languages within the borders of the U.S. The goal of U.S. English is to pass a constitutional amendment designating English as the official language of the U.S.A. Beyond the declaration of official status, the practical purposes of such an amendment would include the elimination of multilingual ballots, the restriction of bilingual education, and the raising of language proficiency standards for citizenship requirements.

As the movement grows, philosophical sides are taken and legal battles are fought. While the English-only promoters argue that a climate of language pluralism would result in a culturally and linguistically divided nation, opponents of this movement charge that the actual basis of U.S. English and other such groups is prejudice against new immigrant groups. They argue that the imposition of an amendment to enforce language standards would serve only to increase prejudice toward non–English speaking groups and further divide ethnic communities within the nation. As evidence that a constitutional amendment is not necessary to promote the learning of English, they put forth the country's history of immigration as an example—assimilation, both cultural and linguistic, has evolved among the nation's immigrant groups naturally, without the existence of a legal statute. In some cases where a state has instituted a law designating English as the official language, court cases have resulted. For example, Arizona made English the official law, requiring that all state and local business be conducted in English only. A state insurance claims manager legally challenged this law, fearing that if she tried to communicate with clients or co-workers in Spanish, her job would be in jeopardy. While the state courts upheld the English-only law, a federal judge struck it down on the grounds that it deprived the employee of her right to freedom of speech.

QUESTIONS

1. Does the U. S. have a legally declared official language? _____

2. Do individual states have laws that make English their official language? _____

3. What is the goal of U.S. English?

   _____

   _____

4. What might be some results of passing a constitutional amendment to make English the official language of the United States?

   _____

   _____

5. Why do some groups believe we need such an amendment?

   _____

   _____

6. Why are some people opposed to such an amendment?

   _____

   _____

7. What were the results of the insurance claims manager's legal case in Arizona?

    _____

    _____

8. What is your opinion about the declaration of English as the official language of the United States?

    _____

    _____

FINAL TEAM TASK: DEBATING THE ISSUE

As a group you will present a debate in which you put forth an education plan for the nonnative speakers of English in your school district. Divide the class into two teams: Pro and Con. In your team do the following:

1. Each team member should play one of the following roles in arguing the team's case:
    - a teacher in a bilingual program
    - a teacher in an English-only program
    - a professor who has conducted research in the area of language-learning
    - a student who is in either a bilingual or an English-only program
    - the recently immigrated parent of a school-age child
2. Choose a moderator who will be neutral, that is, will not argue for either side.
3. Read the background information for your side. Do NOT read the background description for the other team.
4. Prepare an argument approximately 3 minutes long for the debate.
5. Follow the procedure below when conducting the debate:

    A. The Pro team begins with a three-minute presentation.
    B. The Con team then gives a three-minute presentation.
    C. The Pro team gives a three-minute response to the Con team's presentation.
    D. The Con team gives a three-minute response to the Pro team's presentation.
    E. The moderator summarizes and evaluates the strengths of both arguments.

PRO TEAM

You will present an education plan that emphasizes a bilingual program for students whose native language is not English. Consider the following issues in preparing your arguments:

- Current linguistic theory suggests that children learn best if they develop thinking and conceptual skills in their native language.
- Academic achievement test scores have risen in schools that have adopted bilingual programs.
- The academic content taught in English-only programs must be over simplified for the nonnative speakers of English.

CON TEAM

You will present an education plan that emphasizes an English–only program for students whose native language is not English. Consider the following issues in preparing your arguments:

- In large urban school districts there are immigrant students representing more than twenty different native languages; it would, therefore, be impractical to offer bilingual programs for all children.
- The history of the United States itself offers proof that children learn English by being immersed in an all English-speaking environment.
- Immigrant children's ability to learn English and thus fit into the mainstream community is slowed down by being taught in their native language, isolated from children except those of their own native background.

FINAL WRITTEN TASK

Write a 3–5 paragraph essay in which you give your opinion about either:

A. bilingual education versus English-only classes
B. the need to make English legally the official U.S. language.

Your essay can be organized as follows:

1. The first paragraph should be introductory. It should get the reader's attention, introduce the reader to the issue, and give a one-sentence statement of your opinion.
2. The next part should support your opinion and convince the reader why your opinion is sound. In 1–3 paragraphs, develop your opinion by giving reasons and evidence for support.
3. The final paragraph should include a brief summary of what you stated in the middle of your essay and give a strong conclusive statement to convince the reader of the validity of your opinion.

Segment 8

Judgement Day

Oakwood High

Grade Average B

SAT's 1000

from *Primetime Live*, 4/12/90
Runtime: 14:09
Begin:1:18:19

Previewing

KEY QUESTIONS

1. What do high school students have to do to apply to a U.S. university or college?
2. What qualifications do universities consider to be important?
3. What can an applicant do to improve his or her chances of being accepted by a university or college?

DISCUSSION

1. Is it difficult to get accepted to a university in your country? Explain your answer.

_____

_____

2. What do universities in your country consider to be the most important factors when they choose applicants for acceptance?

_____

_____

3. Is higher education expensive in your country? If so, how do students afford to go to college?

_____

_____

PREDICTION

What do you think students have to do to complete the application process for a U.S. college or university? List your predictions below. Confirm your predictions after you have watched the entire segment once.

1. _____

2. _____

3. _____

4. _____

ESSENTIAL WORDS TO KNOW

The *italicized* words in the sentences below are used in the video. Read the sentences and then match the words with their meanings from the list.

a. an average of all grades received
b. a school function a student participates in in addition to classes
c. decision to accept a student on the condition that another student already accepted does not attend
d. letters written about a student's achievements or character and submitted as part his or her application
e. a standardized test required by many universities for admission
f. an essay an applicant writes stating his or her reasons for wanting to attend a particular college

_____ 1. Many students find that writing their *statement of purpose* is the most difficult part of the application process.
_____ 2. The *Scholastic Aptitude Test* (SAT) includes both a math and a verbal section.
_____ 3. High school students who want to continue their studies begin to worry about their *grade point average (GPA)*.
_____ 4. An applicant who is put on a *wait list* still has a chance of getting accepted at the college of her choice.

_____ 5. Most colleges or universities require three *letters of recommendation* for each applicant.

_____ 6. Participation in an *extracurricular activity* such as the Debate Club can improve a student's chances of getting accepted at a university.

Global Viewing

GETTING THE GENERAL IDEA

Read the statements below. Then watch this part of the segment. Who says what? Check (✓) the appropriate column.

01:18:35-
01:26:43

	Josh	Jason	Nina
1. What is college going to look like? What kind of people am I going to run into?	____	____	____
2. In college books, it says that at Kenyon, an interview is highly recommended.	____	____	____
3. Do you go to a lot of parties here, Vanessa? Are you partying a lot?	____	____	____
4. I was vice president of the marching band this year.	____	____	____
5 I want a medium-sized school, definitely. Something manageable.	____	____	____
6. What I like to do, I like to write. And I'm confident when I write.	____	____	____
7. As far as SAT scores go, I didn't do bad on my SATs.	____	____	____
8. Well, last year, they were really bad. I got, like, 800.	____	____	____

PREDICTING THE OUTCOME

Based on your first impression of the three candidates, what do you predict the admissions committee will decide for each? First, check (✓) the appropriate column. Then watch this part of the segment and circle your predictions that were correct.

01:26:44-
01:32:00

	ACCEPT	REJECT	WAIT LIST
Josh	____	____	____
Jason	____	____	____
Nina	____	____	____

Intensive Viewing

GETTING THE IMPORTANT INFORMATION

01:20:15-
01:26:43

Watch this part of the segment and fill in as much information as you can about the three applicants in the chart below.

	JOSH	JASON	NINA
GRADE AVERAGE			
SAT's			
EXTRA-CURRICULAR ACTIVITIES			
LETTERS OF RECOMMENDATION			
OTHER IMPORTANT INFORMATION			

CHECKING YOUR COMPREHENSION

01:26:44-
01:32:20

Read the following sentences. Then watch the second half of the segment. As you watch, decide whether each sentence is true or false. Write *T* or *F*.

_____ 1. Jason's interview was helpful because it proved that he had good reading skills.

_____ 2. Josh was accepted because of his high verbal score and well-written essay.

_____ 3 Josh's soccer skills proved helpful.

_____ 4. Josh received $4,000 in financial aid.

_____ 5. Nina's grades were good throughout her senior year.

_____ 6. Nina was not accepted at any of the colleges she applied to.

Language Focus

UNDERSTANDING IDIOMS

Guess the meaning of the *italicized* idiom in each sentence. Then choose
the statement that has the most similar meaning to the original sentence.

1. Like Nina and Jason, Josh is *no sure bet.*
   a. Nina and Jason will definitely be accepted.
   b. Only Josh will definitely be accepted.
   c. Neither Nina, Jason, nor Josh will definitely be accepted.
2. Together with a strong interview, Josh could still be *in the game.*
   a. Josh will need a strong interview to be accepted.
   b. Josh's interview won't help to get him accepted.
   c. Josh won't be accepted because he didn't play the interview game.
3. Teachers' personal recommendations are *a dime a dozen.*
   a. Applicants to college need dozens of teachers' recommendations.
   b. Teachers' personal recommendations are easy to obtain.
   c. It is not expensive to obtain teachers' personal recommendations.
4. Some things are *better left unsaid.*
   a. Some things should be discussed openly.
   b. Some things shouldn't be discussed at all.
   c. Some things should be mentioned only briefly.
5. I don't want to go *out on a limb* to recommend this student.
   a. I would recommend this student without any hesitation.
   b. I absolutely would not want to recommend this student.
   c. I have some doubts about recommending this student.

EXPRESSING YOUR OPINION

Look at the sentences below which are used to argue for a candidate.

1. Arguing for a candidate
   a. Her verbal score *is fairly strong.*
   b. *I was impressed with* his letters of recommendation.
   c. Because of his soccer skills, *we might want to give him/her a little more consideration.*

Work in pairs. Ask each other for an opinion about each of the three candidates—Josh, Jason and Nina. Use the *italicized* phrases on page 89 to argue for each candidate. Look at the following example.

Question: What do you think about Jason?
Response: *I was impressed with* his interest in literature.

1. Question: _____?
   Response: _____.

2. Question: _____?
   Response: _____.

3. Question: _____?

   Response: _____.

Follow the same procedure used in 1 above in 2 and 3 below.

2. Expressing doubt about a candidate
   a. *I am concerned about* his verbal ability.
   b. *I wonder if* she is really a serious student.

1. Question: _____?
   Response: _____.

2. Question: _____?

   Response: _____.

3. Question: _____?
   Response: _____.

3. Arguing against a candidate
   a. *I did not think that* his essay was very sophisticated.
   b. *I'm afraid that* she'll have trouble competing at Kenyon College.

1. Question: _____?
   Response: _____.

2. Question: _____?
   Response: _____.

3. Question: _____?
   Response: _____.

Postviewing

COMPARING CULTURES

Discuss the following questions in small groups.

1. Were you surprised or shocked by anything you learned from this video?
2. What aspect of applying to a U.S. college or university seems the most difficult to you? Why?
3. Which application system do you prefer, that used in your country or that in the United States? Why?

RELATED READING

Following are fictitious application essays, letters of recommendation, and other application information for four candidates applying to Canyon College. As you read the essays and letters, imagine that you are an admissions counselor at Canyon College and consider each candidate's positive and negative points. When reading the application essays be sure to look for spelling and other mistakes the applicants may have made.

Candidate #1: Jim Brown

Citizenship: U.S.
Gender: M
Marital status: S
Ethnic origin: White, non-Hispanic
Intended field of study: Education

High school GPA: C
SAT score: 950
TOEFL: N/A
Status: Incoming freshman

Application Essay: Jim Brown

Hi, allow me to introduce myself. I'm Jim Brown, varsity football linebacker for the Battle Creek Bulldogs and future physical education coach. I never really wanted to go to college until I met my high school coach, Butch Bagley. He's an inspiration to all of us, and a really great guy! Needless to say, he really turned my life around. When I met Butch and first started talking to him about how he became a coach, I realized that we had a lot in common and that I should really rethink the idea of going to college after all. It was then that I first thought of applying to Canyon College. In regards to my future, I really want to help kids and coach them. I truly believe that being a team player is important in life, and that as a coach I can help kids learn this lesson. I know I can be a great team player for Canyon College, even if my grades in high school don't show it all the time. I promise to give my studies my best shot! Thanks for hearing me out.

Letter of Recommendation for Jim Brown

Dear Admissions Committee,

As Jim Brown's coach for the past 3 years at Battle Creek High School, I have the highest regard for his ability to work as a team player. He always got along well with his teammates, and showed leadership qualities. He's very disciplined. I realize that Jim's grades are a bit below average for a college applicant. However, during his high school years he spent a lot of time training, and was unable to apply himself 100% to his studies. I am sure that he can make the grade at Canyon College, and I know that he has the necessary qualities to become a high school coach, which is his career goal.

Sincerely,

Butch Bagley

Butch Bagley
Coach, Battle Creek High

Candidate #2: Susan McGuire

Citizenship: U.S.
Gender: F
Marital status: S
Ethnic origin: White, non-Hispanic
Intended field of study: History

High school GPA: B
SAT scores: 1300
TOEFL: N/A
Status: Incoming freshman

Application Essay: Susan McGuire

I welcome this opportunity to explain to members of the Selection Committee my reasons for applying to Canyon College. As I've indicated in the application, I intend to major in History, with a minor in English. These are areas not only of personal strength, as can be seen in my high school transcripts, but also disciplines which I find particularly intriguing. As regards the study of History, I am of the belief that we can best understand our modern era and what the future will bring if we have genuine insights into the past and understand the cyclical nature of history. I further believe that the study of the English language and its literature complements the study of history and allows us further insights into our own culture. For these reasons, I am particularly excited about the prospect of studying these subjects at Canyon College, and sincerely hope that the Committee will give me a chance to realize this dream.

You may have noticed in looking over my academic records that my grades in high school are somewhat inconsistent. While I cannot excuse these grades, I feel that the academic environment in my high school did not always motivate or challenge me in ways which I would have liked it to. I believe my high school history grades, my letters of recommendation, and my SAT scores attest to my ability to pursue studies at Canyon, and I sincerely believe that given the academic stimulation which I require, I will be able to apply myself and excel in my chosen areas of study.

Thank you for giving me this chance to express myself.

Letter of Recommendation for Susan McGuire

Dear Canyon College Admissions Committee,

I teach history at Oak Park High School, and have known Susan McGuire since she was a freshman at our school. I am pleased to write this letter of recommendation for her, as she is a gifted student whose intellectual capabilities will easily enable her to succeed in university studies. Although Susan's grades in some of her other subject matter classes here at Oak Park High fell below those in her History classes, I am confident that she is serious about pursuing her studies in History at the university level, and believe that she can rise to the challenge academically. My own assessment of Susan is that she was somewhat bored at high school, and thus did not put much into her studies in classes which did not interest her. Once in a stimulating environment such as Canyon College, I believe that Susan will bloom, and will not disappoint you with her achievements.

Sincerely,

Cecilia Bloomfield

Cecilia Bloomfield
History teacher, Oak Park USD

Candidate #3: Andrew Johnson

Citizenship: U.S.
Gender: M
Marital status: S
Ethnic origin: Black, non-Hispanic
Intended field of study: Education

High school GPA: B+
SAT scores: 1000
TOEFL: N/A
Status: Incoming freshman

Application Essay: Andrew Johnson

This application to Canyon College is the culmination of a long-standing dream of mine—to obtain a college degree and to bring the knowledge I gain in my studies back to my inner city community. To many, the dream of a college education may appear rather mundane; yet for an inner city youth like myself growing up amidst poverty, drugs, and crime, it is a sincere vision for the future—and at present a distant dream rather than a reality. Perhaps some personal information about me may be of interest at this point. I am a senior at Grover Cleveland High School in South Chicago, am the editor of our high school newspaper, *The Final Word*, and will present the valedictory address at the senior graduation this June. In my junior year, I served as Class Treasurer, and have been active in intramural sports on the basketball team throughout my high school career.

A particular interest of mine has always been helping children improve their basic educational skills. When I was elementary school age, my mother enrolled me in a neighborhood tutoring project; I attribute a large degree of my own academic success to the head start which this program provided me. In eighth grade, the Coordinator of this project, Mr. Gregory Culver, approached me to serve as a tutor for younger children—an opportunity which I welcomed. I am currently completing my fifth year as a peer mentor in this program, and intend to continue to work in some capacity with this program during the summer break while I am attending college. As you may have noticed in my application, I have indicated an interest in Education, with the career goal of becoming a secondary school teacher. I am committed to improving education in inner city schools, and would request placement at a school in the immediate environment where I grew up.

Please consider my application carefully; I sincerely hope that I will be given a chance to study at Canyon College.

Letter of Recommendation for Andrew Johnson

Dear members of the Admissions Committee,

I am proud to support Andrew Johnson for admission to Canyon College. He's a terrific individual who has spent the last four years volunteering his time with us at the Upward Bound Program to teach reading and basic math skills to the kids in the community. I'm sure you know how unusual this amount of dedication is in someone of Andrew's age.

Our neighborhood children need more role models like Andrew—college graduates who are committed to coming back into the community and allowing it to benefit from the training they have received. We here at the Upward Bound Program all love and respect Andrew deeply, and know that he will apply himself and succeed in his studies at Canyon College. If you have any further questions, please don't hesitate to contact me.

Sincerely,

Greg Culver

Greg Culver,
Coordinator, Upward Bound Program
Chicago, Illinois

Candidate #4: Juan Rodriguez

Citizenship: Colombian
Gender: M
Marital status: M
Ethnic origin: Hispanic
(junior)
Intended field of study: Computer Science

High school GPA: B+
SAT scores: 950
TOEFL: 500
Status: Transfer student

Application Essay: Juan Rodriguez

Most esteem professors of Canyon College,

In my native country, Colombia, I am university student with honors at the Universidad de Bogota. I study the administration of business and commerce and I desire to study about computers at your university. Computers are the promise of the future, and I am always interesting in them. In my city, I am one of the firsts persons to establish a retail computer software business. This business, La Esquina de Computadores, has now eight stores in Bogota and one in Medellin. I plan in the future open another store in Cartagena and what the future brings, we hope even more. Is very important for me, learn everything about computers. For this reason, I look to the United States and to Canyon College, because this country is advance in technology and I can improve myself and my family situation if you can offer me this opportunity. Please to accept me in your program of Computer Science. I will be honor to be in your college, Canyon. Thank you.

Letter of Recommendation for Juan Rodriguez.

Dear admissions committee members,

Juan Rodriguez was enrolled in the English language program at the Centro Colomboamericano in Bogota this past semester. He participated actively in the TOEFL preparation class which was offered two evenings a week; in addition, he was enrolled in a non-credit conversation course for intermediate-level students. Rodrigo was a motivated student in both these classes. I personally was his teacher in the TOEFL preparation class, and although he did not advance as rapidly as some other students in the class, I felt that he was sincere in his desire to learn English and applied himself to his studies.

I know that Juan is very interested in pursuing studies in Computer Programming in the United States. I wish him luck in this venture.

Sincerely,

Maria Aguirre de Vasquez

Maria Aguirre de Vasquez
EFL Instructor, Centro Colomboamericano
Bogota

FINAL TEAM TASK

You are members of the admissions committee at Canyon College and must decide who to accept for the coming academic year. To do this, you should carefully review all four candidates' application packets, which include pertinent personal information, the candidates' application statements, and one letter of recommendation for each applicant. Because you have an unusually high number of applicants this year, you will be able to accept only two candidates. In your committee meeting, decide:

1. which two applicants you will accept
2. which you will reject
3. if you wish to wait list any of the applicants

All members of the committee must agree. Be prepared to defend your decision with the information you have available.

FINAL WRITTEN TASK

OPTION A

You have now had the chance to examine four sample college application essays and to discuss their strengths and weaknesses. Apply what you have learned and write your own application essay. The instructions below, which are given to the applicants writing an application essay, will guide you.

Application Essay: The essay enables the admissions committee to evaluate your ability to express yourself in writing. The committee will look at your writing style and language usage as well as the organization of your statement. But the importance of the essay goes beyond its mechanics. The essay provides us with information about you as a person—information that cannot be gained through objective data such as grades and test scores. We hope through the essay to discover what it is that makes you exceptional. Please do not write more than one page.

OPTION B

Write a one– to two–page essay in which you compare and contrast the procedure for applying to a college or university in your country with that of a U.S. college or university.

Segment 9

Cheating in College

from *Nightline*, 4/16/90
Runtime: 9:11
Begin: 1:32:32

Previewing

KEY QUESTIONS

1. How common is cheating by college and university students?
2. Why do some students cheat?
3. Is anything being done about cheating in college?

DISCUSSION

1. What methods do students use to cheat that you know of?

   _____

   _____

2. How do teachers in your culture respond when a student is caught cheating?

   _____

   _____

3. Do you think that cheating in school is a very serious "crime"? Why or why not?

   _____

   _____

PREDICTION

Based on the title *Cheating in College* and what you already know about this topic, make predictions about the items below. Confirm your predictions after you have watched the entire segment once.

1. Percentage of college students who cheat: _____

2. Methods of cheating: _____

    _____

3. Students' attitude toward cheating: _____

    _____

ESSENTIAL WORDS TO KNOW

The *italicized* words in the sentences below are used in the video segment. Read the words as they are used in the sentences and try to come up with your own definition.

1. As the teacher was reading Ted's paper, she thought that it sounded very much like an article she had read in the newspaper, so she decided she had better explain to the class that *plagiarism* is a serious crime.

    plagiarism: _____

2. Cheating in academia is considered *unethical* behavior.

    unethical: _____

3. At the end of the quarter or semester, many students stay up several nights in a row to finish writing their *term papers*.

    term paper: _____

4. After studying all night, I ran off to history class to take the *final*.

    final: _____

5. Some people take university courses for fun after they have graduated and no longer need academic *credit*.

    credit: _____

6. The city *commissioned* a sculptor to create a sculpture to stand in front of City Hall.

    commission: _____

Global Viewing

GETTING THE GENERAL IDEA

Read the following statements. Then watch the entire segment and decide whether each sentence is true or false. Write *T* or *F*.

01:32:38-
01:45:55

_____ 1. Cheating in college has decreased in recent years.

_____ 2. Professor Hale was surprised by the results of the survey he conducted.

_____ 3. The students who were interviewed were very ashamed because they had cheated.

_____ 4. Students can buy completed term papers.

_____ 5. Kathy planned to turn in the paper she bought for a class she was taking at UCLA.

_____ 6. Barton Lowe, the owner of Research Assistance, claims that he sells term papers.

_____ 7. District Attorney Ira Reiner says that the company Research Assistance is illegally selling term papers.

_____ 8. When students see other students cheating, they feel justified in cheating also.

Intensive Viewing

GETTING THE IMPORTANT INFORMATION

Read over the questions below. Then circle the correct answer as you listen to this part of the segment.

01:33:55-
01:40:04

1. Diogenes, from Greek mythology, carried a gold lantern through Athens in search of _____.
    a. a mad cynic
    b. a college student
    c. an honest man
    d. both a nd b

2. A survey has recently shown that more college students now cheat but are _____.
    a. not embarrassed
    b. not punished
    c. punished
    d. both a and b

3. Professor Hale's survey revealed that more than _____.
    a. 90 percent of students cheated
    b. 80 percent of students cheated
    c. 60 percent of students cheated
    d. 50 percent of students cheated

4. Which of the following responses was NOT given as a reason for cheating in college?
   a. Pressure from fellow students.
   b. Pressure from family expectations.
   c. You have to do whatever is necessary to succeed.
   d. It's like a crutch.

5. The company Research Assistance advertises _____.
   a. tutors for college students
   b. final exams
   c. college textbooks
   d. research papers

6. Before paying for the research paper, Kathy asked whether it _____.
   a. had been handed in at UCLA
   b. had been written by a UCLA student
   c. had a bibliography
   d. had been plagiarized

7. Kathy was asked to sign a form which said that she _____.
   a. was not a student at UCLA
   b. was not going to sell the paper on campus
   c. was not going to turn the paper in for credit
   d. was not going to pay with a credit card

8. The owner of Research Assistance compares his company to _____.
   a. a bookstore
   b. a library
   c. a research center
   d. a student workshop

9. The District Attorney of Los Angeles believes that Research Assistance _____.
   a. should not be allowed to stay in business
   b. is like a library
   c. offers students assistance
   d. none of the above

10. The District Attorney of Los Angeles has _____.
    a. been investigating Research Assistance
    b. filed legal charges against Research Assistance
    c. violated a California legal code
    d. none of the above

LISTENING CLOZE

Listen to this part of the segment and fill in the missing words. Then compare your answers with those of another student.

James Walker: At Miami University in Oxford, Ohio, _____ are getting ready for the school's 151st graduation. It will be a moment of _____ for the students and their families, a time of professional pride for _____ and _____. But that spirit of achievement here in America's heartland has been shattered by this: a _____ that shows that nine out of ten students cheat.

1st Miami student: This has definitely hurt the _____ a lot, I'd say.

2nd Miami student: You have to, you know, think for your _____, and if the future is grades, then I guess you've got to do what you have to do to _____.

Prof. Jerold Hale: I was very _____ _____ the results. The things that I had read in other studies had indicated that cheating of all sorts, _____ also, were increasing, but I never expected to find the _____ that we did.

James Walker: Prof. Jerold Hale conducted the _____ survey, which revealed that 91 percent of 234 students said they had _____ their college work in some way.

Language Focus

PARAPHRASING STRATEGIES

Paraphrasing means using your own words to express someone else's ideas. Any ideas, written or spoken, that you include in an essay or paper must be expressed in your own words unless you are quoting someone directly. Therefore, if you want to use ideas that you have read, you have to change the way they are expressed while not changing the meaning of the original idea. It is not easy for students whose native language is English to paraphrase well, and it is an even more difficult task for nonnative speakers of English. Some guidelines to help you learn to paraphrase are given on page 102.

For each pair of sentences, underline the word or words in *A* that are changed in *B* and circle the similar words used in *B*.

1. Change vocabulary items
   A. A common form of cheating is purchasing term papers.
   B. A common type of cheating is buying research papers.

2. Change a word into a phrase, or a phrase into a word
   A. Most companies that sell research papers promise the buyers confidentiality.
   B. Most companies that sell research papers promise not to reveal the identities of the buyers.
   A. Juniors and seniors, as well as freshmen and sophomores, have been found to cheat.
   B. Upperclassmen, as well as freshmen and sophomores, have been found to cheat.

3. Change from active to passive, or passive to active
   A. The owner of Research Assistance claims that his company doesn't sell any research papers.
   B. The owner of Research Assistance claims that no research papers are sold by his company.
   A. A form is signed by the buyer that says he will not turn the paper in for academic credit.
   B. The buyer signs a form that says he will not turn the paper in for academic credit.

4. Change the word form
   A. With 90 percent of college students cheating, one might wonder what has happened to academic standards.
   B. With 90 percent of college students cheating, one might wonder what has happened to standards in academia.

PRACTICE PARAPHRASING
Try to use each of the four methods explained above to write paraphrases of the following sentences. (There are many possible ways to paraphrase each sentence.)

1. Students and professors were shocked by the results of a recent survey.

   _____

   _____

2. The survey revealed that 90 percent of students in college cheat.

_____

_____

3. It was also surprising that the students interviewed did not feel guilty about cheating on tests or plagiarizing term papers.

_____

_____

4. Companies even sell completed term papers to students who can turn them in for academic credit.

_____

_____

EXPRESSING PROBABILITY AND GIVING ADVICE

Read the situations below. For each case think about how the person described *must feel* or *must have felt* in that situation. Then consider what he or she *should do* or *should have done*. After writing your answers in the space provided, compare them with others in small groups.

SITUATION A

Sarah had a 10–page paper due for her history class on Monday. It was Sunday afternoon, and she hadn't even started working on the paper. She called up her friend Joe and mentioned the situation she was in. Joe said, "No problem. I wrote a paper two years ago that you can use if you want. It was on the Civil War. " Sarah felt immediately relieved. The topic was perfect. She got the paper from Joe, erased his name, and replaced it with her own. Then she photocopied it and handed it in to the professor on Monday. A week later as the professor was handing back the papers, she told the class that Sarah's paper was exactly what she had wanted. She asked Sarah if it would be ok for the other students to read her paper as an example of an excellent term paper. Sarah turned red and said it would be fine.

How must Sarah have felt?

_____

_____

What should she have done in this situation?

_____

_____

SITUATION B

John is taking a final exam in Economics. Although Economics has not been an easy class for him, John has been working hard all semester for this class. He studied five hours yesterday for this test, and he feels very confident that he will do well. The person sitting next to him hardly ever attended class. Now he keeps looking at John's answers and copying from his test. He even asked John a question about one of his answers.

How must John feel?

_____

_____

What should John do?

_____

_____

SITUATION C

An important exam was taking place for all English as a Second Language students. The results of the test would determine whether the students could take regular university classes. The teacher who was proctoring the exam noticed that one student kept looking at the bottom of his shoe. As the teacher watched this student more closely, he noticed that the student had a paper with writing taped to the bottom of his shoe. The teacher went to the student's desk, took the student's test and ripped it up, and then asked the student to leave.

How must the student have felt?

_____

_____

What should the teacher have done?

_____

_____

What should the student have done after this incident?

_____

_____

SITUATION D

Anna attended a prestigious Ivy League university and majored in Anthropology. She had been a straight A student and graduated with honors. After graduation she spent several months looking for a job. Unfortunately, she couldn't find a job that was intellectually challenging or for which she would be able to use the knowledge and skills she had acquired in school. Now, although she hasn't given up looking for a suitable job, she has begun to work as a waitress to pay her rent. Today she saw a job advertised that sounded interesting. The desired person for this job must have excellent research skills and writing ability. Anna called the number and inquired about the job. She found out that the company is called Research Associates. They hire people to write research papers that university students can buy and hand in for credit. When the employer heard about Anna's educational background, he was very interested in hiring her. He even offered her a salary that is three times as much as she's making as a waitress. Anna can't decide whether she should work for a company whose ethics she is so opposed to. However, she is also very sick of being a waitress.

How must Anna feel?

_____

_____

What should she do?

_____

_____

Postviewing

COMPARING CULTURES

Discuss the following questions in small groups.

1. Were you surprised or shocked by anything you learned from this video?

2. The attitudes expressed about cheating by the students in this video suggest that cheating is not taken very seriously, at least by many U.S. college or university students. Do you think cheating is taken more or less seriously by university students in your country? Explain further.

3. In the United States plagiarism is considered a serious offense, both for students and for people in public or political offices. Is plagiarism a serious offense in your country? Explain further.

4. Do companies like Research Assistance exist in your country? If so, is there any question about their legality? Do you think such companies should be allowed? Why or why not?

RELATED READING

Read the article *Putting an End to Cheating* and answer the questions that follow.

Putting an End to Cheating

Two computer programs have been developed that can help put an end to dishonesty in the classroom. David Harpp and James Hogan, chemistry professors at McGill University, Montreal, Canada, also recommend routine use of random seating and multiple-version exams to eliminate cheating that they estimate may reach at least 5 percent for any given sitting.

Harpp indicates that universities have a moral obligation to prevent classroom cheating because it causes ethical and intellectual damage. "It punishes good students who work hard." When he analyzed test results of 1,000 students from two entry-level science classes, he found that about 50 of them probably had cheated. The study concluded that at least a 5 percent level of cheating takes place on multiple-choice exams. This was confirmed by analysis of test papers from other disciplines and from outside McGill University. "The basis for the detection of cheating is the 'mental fingerprints' students leave when they copy from one another. These fingerprints or patterns can easily be detected by statistical methods," which is the basis for his computer programs.

"The computer programs compare and consider the probability of pairs of students getting the same answers. Answer sheets of all pairs of students are checked, and those with a predefined number of differences in their papers are flagged." In all cases, the programs look at the number of wrong answers students have in common, as well as the number they answered in the same way. "If the ratio of one to the other exceeds a certain value, the pair of students are targeted as suspects." In every case he looked at, those students sat in close proximity to one another in the exam room.

Cheating on multiple-choice tests was eliminated completely when students were seated randomly and/or multiple versions of the exams were passed out. Harpp recommends that these common-sense measures should be used for all exams and by all universities. Seating charts also should be kept for reference because they could serve as supporting evidence if two tests were considered "suspect," he suggests. "Assigning random and widely spaced seating patterns also reduces incentives for cheating by preventing close friends from sitting together."

*Reprinted with permission from *USA TODAY Periodical*, April 1991.

QUESTIONS

1. What three things does Professor Harpp recommend that universities do to eliminate cheating on multiple-choice exams?

   _____

   _____

2. According to Professor Harpp, who gets hurt by cheating?

   _____

   _____

3. The professors' study was conducted on one kind of test-taking situation. What kind of exam was involved in their study?

   _____

   _____

4. What percentage of students cheat on any given multiple-choice exam?

   _____

   _____

5. What does Professor Harpp mean when he refers to the "mental fingerprints" students leave when cheating?

   _____

   _____

6. Do you agree with Harpp's recommendations to cut down on cheating? Why or why not?

   _____

   _____

FINAL TEAM TASK: A UNIVERSITY TASK FORCE ON CHEATING

You are members of a small (3 to 6 member) university task force formed to determine the university's policy on academic cheating. The task force is made up of 1 or 2 student representatives, 1 or 2 professors, and 1 or 2 university administrators. Due to the recent publicity about the incredibly high percentage of students who cheat, your university faces a hostile public that wonders why their tax dollars should support such an unethical institution. Your task is to draft a statement that expresses the university's policy on cheating. Included in the statement should be:

1. an introductory statement voicing your concern about the issue
2. a statement about how you will deal with cheating, including specific policies about copying on tests and plagiarizing of papers
3. a concluding statement to convince the public that you are taking steps to solve the problem

Present your prepared statement to the rest of the class. Then as a class decide which policy you think is best.

FINAL WRITTEN TASK

OPTION A

Write a one–paragraph summary of the article *Putting an End to Cheating*. In writing a summary, you are expressing the important ideas of an article in your own words. Therefore, you must paraphrase what another writer has stated without plagiarizing. Use the guidelines on paraphrasing that you learned in the Language Focus section on pages 101–102 to help you write your summary. It is also helpful to keep in mind several other criteria for writing a summary.

1. Include all the important points.
2. Do not include unimportant points like examples, details, or short quotations.
3. Do not include information that is not in the original article, such as related theories or your own opinion.

OPTION B

Write an opinion paper in which you either defend or oppose the right for a company that sells research papers to exist. Consider the following questions before you begin to write:

1. Is the company doing something that is simply unethical or should it be illegal?
2. Who is actually committing an offense, the company selling the papers or the students who are buying the papers and handing them in as their own work for academic credit?

Segment 10

New Suburban Designs for Living

from *World News Tonight*, 1/7/92
Runtime: 5:00
Begin: 01:46:06

Previewing

KEY QUESTIONS

1. Why did people begin to move out to the suburbs several decades ago?
2. What has gone wrong with the suburban lifestyle?
3. What aspects of suburban living could be improved?
4. How might a newly designed suburb differ from the traditional suburb?

DISCUSSION

1. What do you think people imagine the "suburban dream" to be?

    _____

    _____

2. What are suburbs like in your country? What are some problems associated with them?

    _____

    _____

3. Have you ever had a chance to visit or live in a U.S. suburb? If so, how did it compare to suburbs in your own country?

    _____

    _____

PREDICTION

Based on the title of this segment, *New Suburban Designs for Living* and the ideas you have discussed so far, make predictions about how a reinvented suburb will differ from a traditional suburb. Confirm your predictions after you've watched the entire segment once.

1. _____

2. _____

3. _____

4. _____

ESSENTIAL WORDS TO KNOW

The following words are important words used in the video segment. For each of the sentences below taken from the video, determine which word fits best to complete the sentence.

commute   sprawling   suburbanites   complex (noun)

pedestrians   zoning laws

1. Apple Computer is building a _____ next door.

2. The goal is to bring _____ closer together.

3. They make the streets more narrow so cars slow down and _____ feel safer.

4. Frank begins a two–hour _____ to Los Angeles at 4:30 every morning.

5. In any other suburb, _____ would keep homes and offices far apart.

6. _____ modern suburbs are geared more to cars than community.

Global Viewing

SOUND OFF

01:41:50-
01:43:08

Watch this part of the segment with the sound turned off. Then answer the questions on page 111. When you finish, compare your answers with those of another student. Then watch the segment with the sound on and compare what you wrote with what you hear on the soundtrack.

110

1. What aspect of suburban living is being emphasized during the first part of this section?

   _____

   _____

2. Do you think the man and woman being interviewed are happy with their suburban lifestyle? Why or why not?

   _____

   _____

3. What aspect of suburban living is being emphasized in the later section of the video?

   _____

   _____

GETTING THE MAIN IDEA

Read through the questions below. Then choose the correct answers as you watch the entire segment.

01:41:20-
01:46:00

1. Which of the following are mentioned as problems of the typical suburban lifestyle?
   a. too much driving
   b. not enough time for family
   c. not enough time for friends
   d. all of the above

2. Suburbs leave neighbors isolated from each other because _____.
   a. people want their privacy
   b. the houses are enclosed by fences
   c. the suburbs are designed for cars
   d. all of the above

3. Some new designs for suburbs have more features of _____.
   a. small towns
   b. large cities
   c. European villages
   d. rural areas

4. One plan for a new suburb includes
   a. computers for every home
   b. office buildings near the homes
   c. no individual cars
   d. a modern subway system

5. The appeal of making suburbs more like small towns is that _____.
   a. people will pay more attention to the environment
   b. people are very nostalgic for lost traditions
   c. the environment will be designed with humans in mind
   d. all of the above

Intensive Viewing

LISTENING CLOZE

01:41:20-
01:42:07

Watch this part of the segment again and fill in the blanks with the missing words. Then compare your answers with those of another student.

Peter Jennings: On the American Agenda this evening: _____ _____ the suburbs. For so many people who live in the suburbs, life often seems to be one _____ _____ drive. Someone figured out that members of a typical family in the suburbs get into the car an _____ of thirteen times a day: go to work, _____ _____ the car; get in the car, get the _____ ; get in the car, get the kids. Not much time left over for family, friends, _____. Life in the suburbs can use more than some fine tuning. Our Agenda reporter is Ned Potter.

Ned Potter: Marino Valley, California. The D'Agostino family thought it could find the _____ _____ here, but it turned out to be a nightmare. Frank begins a two–hour _____ to Los Angeles at 4:30 every morning. Margaret has to _____ the kids before she gets to her own job.

112

GETTING THE IMPORTANT INFORMATION

Watch the rest of the segment. Write brief answers to the following questions.

1. What two complaints do the D'Agostinos have about suburban living?

   a. _____

   b. _____

2. What is the one major difference between the new suburb in Seaside, Florida, and traditional suburbs?

   _____

3. What goal did the designers have for the Seaside suburb?

   _____

   _____

4. How did the designers of Seaside plan the community to keep neighbors from being isolated from one another? List three specific things the designers did to achieve this goal.

   a. _____

   b. _____

   c. _____

5. What is the most important aspect of architect Peter Calthorpe's plan for the new community, Laguna West?

   _____

6. What are three of the benefits offered by reinvented suburbs with a small town feel?

   a. _____

   b. _____

   c. _____

Language Focus

MORE USEFUL VOCABULARY

How many of the terms related to homes do you know? Match the definition below with the terms they define.

a. an open-sided shelter for a car often formed by extending the roof over the driveway
b. an opening, like a door, in a fence
c. coverings for windows, often made from wood, that can be closed to form a solid covering.
d. a platform built out from the wall of the upstairs of a house where people can stand or sit
e. a sidewalk leading to the front door of a house
f. a central, interior area of a house or group of houses that is exposed to the open air
g. a raised wooden platform built out from a house often used as an area for outdoor recreation
h. a hollow structure extending from the roof that allows smoke to pass through to the outside
i. a small, private road that leads from the street to a house or garage
j. an outdoor area next to a house that is paved with bricks or stones and used for outdoor recreation
k. a low wall that marks the boundary between a house and the sidewalk or road
l. a cloth or metal covering that protrudes out over a window or door to protect it from rain

_____ 1. balcony	_____ 5. carport	_____ 9. fence
_____ 2. deck	_____ 6. patio	_____ 10. gate
_____ 3. chimney	_____ 7. front walk	_____ 11. courtyard
_____ 4. driveway	_____ 8. awning	_____ 12. shutters

PRACTICE WITH NEW VOCABULARY: YOUR DREAM HOUSE

Imagine the house of your dreams. Which of the features mentioned in the two exercises above would it include?

1. Draw a picture of your dream house.
2. Without letting your partner see the picture you drew, describe the house to your partner. Give a clear description of the house so that he or she can draw it.

3. Compare the picture you drew to the one your partner drew to your instructions.
4. Then change roles; your partner gives you verbal instructions to draw his or her dream house.

Postviewing

COMPARING CULTURES

Discuss the following questions in small groups.

1. Were you surprised or shocked by anything you learned from this video?
2. Many people in the United States still believe in the "suburban dream". What do you think are the benefits they think of when they desire this lifestyle?
3. It has been said that Americans have a love affair with the automobile. Does the video segment support this statement? Explain your answer.
4. Do you think communities like the village of Seaside, Florida, will give residents a better life than typical suburbs like the one in which the D'Agostinos live? In what ways does it or doesn't it offer a better lifestyle?
5. Do suburbs in your country have some of the same problems as those illustrated in this video? How are the problems similar or different?
6. Are either of the "reinvented" suburbs shown in the video—Seaside, Florida, or Laguna West—similar to towns or suburbs in your country? In what ways?

RELATED READING

The article on page 116 looks at two cities' solutions to a problem called "urban sprawl", that is, the spreading of houses and services to the area beyond the city limit. Urban sprawl is actually a process that results in the creation of suburbs.

1. Read the introduction (the first four paragraphs) and then answer the comprehension questions that follow the article.
2. After reading the introduction, half of the students will read Portland, Oregon's, answer to the problem of urban sprawl, and the other half will read Davis, California's, solution. Fill in the grid, Two Solutions to Urban Sprawl, with information from the part that you read.
3. Find a partner who read the part you didn't read. Ask your partner to tell you about the part he or she read so that you can complete the grid.

Creative Alternatives to Urban Sprawl: A Tale of Two Cities
by Todd Oppenheimer

Urban sprawl offers many things that car-oriented Americans have come to expect—fast food, fast roads, and convenient shopping centers. It is also an easy method of creating new subdivisions, sitting just beyond the noise of urban life. But sprawl can also weaken or destroy the vitality of downtowns, limit the supply of inexpensive houses, paralyze the roads with cars, eat away at safe drinking water supplies, and scar much of the landscape with asphalt, plastic signs, and sterile, cookie-cutter buildings. It also perpetuates the automobile as the sole component of our urban transportation system, because it makes alternatives such as mass transit, bicycles, and walking almost impossible.

For some people, sprawl's damages run even deeper, destroying a crucial sense of community. In their book *Sustainable Communities*, Sim Van der Ryn and Peter Calthorpe argue that the modern suburban lifestyle has imprisoned us in a narcissistic world of private property—automobiles, sealed office buildings, shopping centers, and subdivisions. Meanwhile, our shared domains—public parks and plazas, intimate public streets built with neighborhood stores and sidewalks for pedestrians—have been eliminated.

So how do you build a healthy economy and keep a sense of neighborhood? How do you save a downtown? How do you accommodate growth without traffic jams? How do you create affordable housing? And how do you protect your land and water supplies?

To find the answers to these questions, I traveled to Oregon and California, where some of the more ambitious programs to limit urban sprawl are in place.

Portland, Oregon

Twenty years ago, the economy of downtown Portland, Oregon, was as weak as any ailing downtown in the country. Stores were steadily leaving the area, and the streets, they used to say, "closed at 5 p.m." In 1969 the nation's then-largest–regional mall was built across the river that borders downtown Portland, stealing half of downtown's commerce overnight.

Suburbs mushroomed in distant corners of Portland's metropolitan area, pulling more activity from Portland and forcing the city to build more freeways. Traffic was continually contributing to air pollution around Portland, violating federal standards for all but a few months of the year. By 1972, says Bill Wyatt, director of the Association for Portland Progress, "Downtown was clearly on the slide, and going downhill fast. A real crisis atmosphere started."

A year later, Neil Goldschmidt was elected as Portland's mayor and launched a $420 million bus and railway plan. At the same time, Portland halted construction on one of its main expressways along the Willamette River and used much of the highway money for mass transit. In the highway's place, Portland built a waterfront park. Several years later, the city tore down a parking garage that sat on downtown's most valuable piece of real estate. In its place, with $8.5 million, Portland built a facility that doesn't draw a penny of income. It's now a piazza named, appropriately, Pioneer Square.

The overall goal was to do what most city officials fear is impossible: bring people to the center of the city day and night. By the early 1980s, downtown employment had grown by 60 percent.

Walking through Portland one sunny morning, I passed dozens of nooks and crannies, which told me that city planners had carefully thought of me, the pedestrian. City parks and fountains—from the small and cozy to the large and glorious—pop up throughout downtown. An old colonnade facade was saved as a border for Portland's busy Saturday market. Drinking fountains are everywhere.

For lunch I stopped at Pioneer Square and found a hub of activity most communities only dream about. In the center, which is surrounded by an amphitheater, gathered musicians, magicians, and food vendors with pushcarts. I ate my lunch sitting on a long tile ledge that borders the square's waterfall. On the cobblestone street behind me ran Portland's new light rail line, opened in 1987. Almost anytime one can see clusters of people waiting under protected shelters for one of Portland's 500 buses. Each shelter contains a detailed sign of that bus route, a phone, and a TV screen displaying the schedule.

In many growing areas around the country, officials are generally pessimistic about mass transit, saying people refuse to live in patterns centralized enough to make it feasible. But, Portland transit officials note, a range of bus and van systems can be coordinated to fit dispersed communities. And people are willing to change. In Portland, which like many cities struggles with diffused suburban growth, transit officials already have counted $400 million in new private development along the transit lines.

Portland's downtown car traffic now looks like that of a town half its size, and air pollution standards are violated an average of one day a year.

Davis, California

In various corners of the country, old cities have begun downtown revitalizing efforts that may someday result in the kind of life Portland enjoys. But even if they succeed in using mass transit and pedestrian-friendly designs to make their cities less dependent on the auto, that won't keep developments on the fringes of town from turning into sprawl.

The most common approach to fighting such suburban sprawl has involved aggressive building restrictions, such as those in Davis, a quaint college town of 40,000 in the middle of California's farm country. Davis' residents are obsessed with preserving its intimate, college-town flavor. So for more than a decade they have made the unusual choice of putting almost no one on the city council or planning commissions who has financial ties to real estate development. As a result, Davis council members have been able to slow the city's accelerating rate of growth, create a certain amount of low and moderately priced housing, and maintain its peaceful and diverse neighborhood atmosphere.

The mixed approach to housing is a direct result of a 1975 growth control regulation, which involves a point system and a limit on building permits (about 400 per year). Before approving each of those homes, city officials ask for a range of "extras" from developers, such as a diversity of designs, a good supply of less expensive homes, a minimum of environmental damage, creation of open areas, and help with additional city service cost. Those who accumulate the most "points" on these extras are first in line for building permits.

Davis also restricts the size of its shopping centers to eight acres. The idea behind this rule is to create commercial centers that are oriented to each neighborhood, rather than expansive regional monoliths that only compete with each other and feel inhuman to shoppers. Most Davis residents now have to drive (or walk or bicycle) only a mile or so for their basic daily needs. Shopkeepers know their customers. The grid of roads to these scattered centers is rarely jammed. When it's hot, thanks to landscaping regulations, people can park underneath canopies of trees.

Davis' goal, in essence, has been to create an alternative to some of the worst aspects of sprawl.

As in any city, there have been limits to the creativity of city officials. But the community ethic in Davis runs deep, even in some private developers. A local planning consultant, recently elected as the first developer on the city council in more than a decade, built a subdivision in one corner of Davis that is reputed to be one of the most innovative subdivisions in the world. The project, called Village Homes, comprises 240 homes on 62 acres, which are threaded with vineyards, fruit orchards, knolls of wild vegetation, and a network of small parks, and foot, and bicycle paths. Homes sit in tight clusters along narrow streets. And, most unique, the homes back up against the streets in tight, intimate clusters. The front yards open onto the shared common areas of countryside.

*Reprinted with permission from the *Independent Weekly*, October 22, 1987.

COMPREHENSION QUESTIONS

Answer the following questions using information from the first four paragraphs of the article.

1. What things do some people see as benefits of urban sprawl?

   _____

   _____

2. What are some of the problems that urban sprawl brings to cities?

   _____

   _____

3. In what ways does urban sprawl harm our sense of community?

   _____

   _____

TWO SOLUTIONS TO URBAN SPRAWL

	PORTLAND, OREGON	DAVIS, CALIFORNIA
Problems Caused by Urban Sprawl	_____ _____ _____ _____ _____	_____ _____ _____ _____ _____
Changes Made to Solve Problems	_____ _____ _____ _____ _____	_____ _____ _____ _____ _____
Goal City Hoped to Reach	_____ _____ _____ _____ _____	_____ _____ _____ _____ _____
Improvements Since Changes Were Made	_____ _____ _____ _____ _____	_____ _____ _____ _____ _____

FINAL TEAM TASK: PLANNING A NEW COMMUNITY

In small groups, imagine that you are a team of urban planners. Your task is to design a community that will be developed in the area where you are now studying. This means that you must take into consideration the specific environmental conditions of this area. For example, if the area is very cold or rainy, you may want to plan for a way to get from one building to another without freezing or getting wet. Also think about the following questions in planning your community:

- What kind of commercial centers do you want, a downtown area or regional shopping centers?
- What kind of outdoor space should your community have, a large central park with most of the houses surrounding it or several small parks to be used by different neighborhoods?
- Should factories and businesses be located near the homes or in a separate business district?
- What will the main means of transportation be, cars or a mass transit system?
- What other specific features in your plan will give the inhabitants a sense of community?

1. Discuss the kind of community your team wants to plan.
2. Draw a large map of the future community, a map that includes all the important features.
3. Present your plan to the rest of the class, which acts as the city council that will adopt one plan out of all those presented.
4. After all of the plans have been presented, the class (city council) votes on the plan it wants to implement.

FINAL WRITTEN TASK

EXPRESSING YOUR OPINION IN AN ESSAY

Both the video segment and the reading emphasized the idea that today's suburbs lack a sense of community. Do you feel this to be true? Before you begin to answer this questions, think about what specifically is meant by a *sense of community*. Write an essay in which you discuss the meaning of this phrase and express your opinion about whether you feel that a sense of community is lacking in suburbs or cities today. In your essay you do not have to use examples from either the video or the reading; examples from your own experience are valid when writing an opinion essay.

Segment 11

Health Care for the Poor

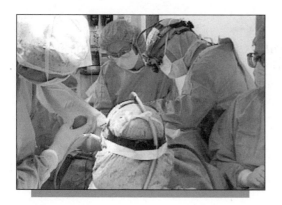

from *World News Tonight*, 10/23/91
Runtime: 5:00
Begin: 01:46:32

Previewing

KEY QUESTIONS

1. What is the best way to ensure that everyone gets health care?
2. Can the government afford to treat all health problems for those who cannot pay for their own health care?
3. Should a government be allowed to rank health problems in order to decide which they can afford to pay for?

DISCUSSION

1. Who pays for your health care in your country?

   _____

   _____

2. How do the unemployed pay for health care in your country?

   _____

   _____

3. Approximately what percentage of a person's salary goes toward taxes in your country? What kind of services do people receive in return?

   _____

   _____

4. Are people generally satisfied with the health care system in your country? Why or why not?

_____

_____

PREDICTION

Based on the title of the segment, *Health Care for the Poor*, the discussion you've had with your classmates, and your own knowledge, what information will be included in this video segment?

1. _____

2. _____

3. _____

4. _____

ESSENTIAL WORDS TO KNOW

The *italicized* words in the sentences below are used in the video. Read the sentences and the definitions. Then write an original sentence for each word.

1. Oregon has a *radical* plan to provide health care for the poor.
   radical = involving major change

   _____

   _____

2. Some medical treatments are *covered by Medicaid*.
   covered by Medicaid = paid for by a government program for the poor

   _____

   _____

3. If you don't pay your insurance bills, your *coverage* will be denied.
   coverage = the state of having an insurance policy provide funds for an individual or family

   _____

   _____

4. Not everyone has *access* to free health care.
   access (noun)= ability to obtain

   _____

   _____

5. With such severe budget problems, the government must *rank* social
   problems in order of importance.
   rank = put in a hierarchical order

   _____

   _____

6. The government gave economic problems high *priority* and education
   issues low *priority*.
   priority = something deserving attention

   _____

   _____

Global Viewing

UNDERSTANDING THE IMPORTANT POINTS

Read the statements below. Then watch the entire segment and decide
whether each statement is true or false. Write *T* or *F*.

01:46:45-
01:51:06

_____ 1. Florida and Oregon both have budget problems.
_____ 2. Florida and Oregon are solving their health care problems in
         similar ways.
_____ 3. Some doctors charge high fees to people even if they are not
         covered by health insurance.
_____ 4. In Oregon few people do not have health insurance.
_____ 5. Medicaid does not provide health care for all poor people.
_____ 6. In Oregon's plan all of the poor will have access to basic
         health care.
_____ 7. In Oregon's plan illnesses are ranked according to their medical
         and social importance.
_____ 8. Oregon's plan is generally accepted by most people.
_____ 9. The federal government has offered an alternative health care
         solution for Oregon to adopt.
_____ 10. At the time this video segment was made, the federal
         government had vetoed Oregon's health care plan.

Intensive Viewing

LISTENING CLOZE

Watch this part of the segment and fill in the blanks with the missing words. Then compare your answers with those of another student.

Peter Jennings: On the American Agenda tonight, a _____ new experiment in providing _____ _____. Last night we reported on the Agenda that the state of Florida, because it is short of money, is removing thousands of poor people from the _____ rolls. In other words, taking medical care away from those who could least _____ it. Tonight, the case of Oregon: same _____ troubles as Florida, but a completely different _____. Our Agenda reporter is Tim Johnson.

GETTING THE FACTS

Watch the rest of the segment and choose the best answer to each of the questions below.

1. The health care plans suggested by Florida and Oregon are discussed because _____.
   a. they are both taking poor people off of Medicaid
   b. Oregon's plan is radically different from Florida's plan
   c. neither state has a serious problem with its health care system
   d. both a and b

2. Oregon's plan would make sure that _____.
   a. the budget problems would be solved
   b. the rich would no longer have access to health insurance
   c. none of the poor would be cut out of the health care system
   d. all of the above

3. Medicaid, the health care system for the poor, is not offered to _____.
   a. single women without children
   b. all men
   c. children over the age of eight
   d. all of the above

4. Under Oregon's proposed system, the following illnesses or conditions would get high priority and probably would be covered for anyone who could not afford to pay:
    a. AIDS
    b. pregnancy
    c. infertility
    d. both a and b

5. One worry about Oregon's health care proposal is that _____.
    a. it is unfair to the rich who already pay high health care costs
    b. it costs too much for the state
    c. the illnesses it covers change depending on the state's yearly budget
    d. they have no other alternative solution

6. Oregon's plan differs from the plans of many other states because _____.
    a. it provides some health care for everyone who needs it
    b. it cuts only the poorest off of Medicaid
    c. it offers the cheapest solution to the problem
    d. it does away with Medicaid entirely

Language Focus

IDENTIFYING CONNECTING PHRASES

In the excerpts from the video segment on page 126, fill in the missing phrases as you listen. Each missing phrase serves as a signal to the listener— it shows the relationship between the sentence or phrase before the connecting phrase and the sentence or phrase after it. In the examples below, the connecting phrase signals that what follows will be either a(n):

explanation: what comes after the connecting phrase will explain in more detail what has been stated before

example: what comes after the connecting phrase will be an example of what has been stated before

restatement: what comes after the connecting phrase states the same meaning as the previous sentence, phrase, or word in a different way

01:46:45-
01:47:00

Peter Jennings: On the American Agenda tonight, a radical new experiment in providing health care. Last night we reported on the Agenda that the state of Florida, because it is short of money, is removing thousands of poor people from the Medicaid rolls, (1) _____ _____ _____ ,taking medical care away from those who could least afford it.

01:48:23-
01:49:40

Dr. Timothy Johnson: Under Oregon's controversial new plan, all of the poor will get basic health care, but to pay for it the state will eliminate their access to some treatments. (2) _____ _____ ____ _____ After 18 months of public hearings, Oregon drew up a list of 709 medical conditions and treatments and ranked them in the order of their medical and social importance. Preventive care and treatable life-threatening conditions are given high priority; minor conditions and incurable diseases are given lower priority. (3) _____ _____ , full treatment of early AIDS infections is high on the list, but intensive care that won't save lives is not. Prenatal and obstetrics care gets high priority, but many infertility treatments do not. With these priorities set, the state then figured out how much money it can spend on health care for the poor each year, which meant drawing the line for the first year at option 587. The net result is that everyone who meets federal poverty guidelines is eligible for any treatment up to that number, (4) _____ treatment for heartburn at 587 would be covered, but disc disease where surgery is not essential at 588 would not be covered.

What does each of the above connecting phrases signal to the listener?

1. _____

2. _____

3. _____

4. _____

126

Postviewing

COMPARING CULTURES

Discuss the following questions in small groups.

1. Were you surprised or shocked by anything you learned from this video?
2. Not only does a high number of people in the United States have no health insurance coverage, but U.S. health care costs are among the highest in the world. Some people think that the government should do something to control the high cost of U.S. health care. Does the government have any control over the cost of health care in your country? If so, do people think this is a good idea? Explain.
3. How do poor people pay for health care in your country?
4. What is considered to be the biggest problem for your country's health care system?

RELATED READING

Read the article *The Health Care Crisis in the United States* and answer the questions that follow.

The Health Care Crisis in the United States

Like an out-of-control epidemic, the health care crisis has been spreading rapidly throughout the country. This crisis strikes the poor, who were once able to get access to doctors through the Medicaid system. Now this system can no longer afford to help all those who need help. The crisis hits the middle-aged hoping to retire, who at one time assumed their employee health insurance policy would continue to cover them until they reached the age of 65, when Medicare would take over. Now many company policies end within weeks of the last day of employment. The crisis touches those who, ironically enough, would seem to need help the most—those covered by health insurance who are unlucky enough to be struck by a serious illness. Today stories abound of AIDS or cancer patients whose insurance companies will no longer cover them because they will simply cost too much. The crisis affects the public hospitals, which are required by law to accept all walk-in emergency cases. These days the emergency rooms are overflowing with patients needing routine medical services for minor ailments like sore throats or the flu who, unable to afford the cost of a doctor's visit, have no other access to medical treatment than through the emergency room.

What are the causes of this crisis of such epidemic proportion? At the root of the problem is the fact that the cost of health care has been sky-rocketing over the past decade. Tied up in the cost of health care are three distinct members of the health care system, all interrelated and each pointing a finger at the others in blame for the tragic state of this system. They are the medical industry, the health insurance industry, and the legal system.

Medical-care prices, including the cost of hospital care and physicians' services, increased at a rate almost twice the rate of inflation during the 1980s. Reflected in these increases is the high cost of new life-saving medical procedures such as organ transplants. Whereas these procedures in previous decades were rare enough to make headlines, they have become almost commonplace today. Sophisticated new medical technology, such as diagnostic procedures including CT scans and Magnetic Resonance Imaging (MRI), is now being used increasingly where formerly X-rays had been used. This new technology is not only superior in its diagnostic power to the previous tools but far more expensive. The cost of developing new life-saving medication and therapies for serious illnesses such as cancer and AIDS is a part of the rising cost of the medical industry as well.

The price of medical care is directly related to the cost of health insurance. Health insurance companies pass on this cost to the consumer in the form of higher premiums (that is, the usual monthly amount the insured pays for a policy), higher deductibles (the amount the insured must pay toward his or her medical expenses before the insurance company begins to cover the bills), and higher out-of-pocket expenses that the insured must cover (these include the percentage of each bill that is the insured's responsibility until his or her medical expenses reach an out-of-pocket limit). Some health insurance companies also exclude coverage of certain expensive medical procedures such as infertility or substance abuse treatment. And in order to maximize their profit margin, many health insurance companies have been trying to minimize the number of high risk cases they cover by not accepting people who have a history of specific medical problems.

A third factor that contributes to the problems is a legal system that makes medical malpractice a constant and extremely expensive fear that no doctor can disregard. The tremendous cost of medical malpractice insurance is represented in the bill the patient receives for his doctor's services. The threat of malpractice suits is responsible for what is known as the practice of defensive medicine by U.S. doctors. The term *defensive medicine* is used to refer to doctors ordering all possible tests and using only the safest procedures in treating patients in order to be covered in the event that he or she may be named the defendant in a malpractice suit.

The complicated, interrelated nature of the medical, health insurance, and legal industries results in the tragic fact that at least 34 million Americans have no health insurance whatsoever. In addition to this, many more who believe they are fully covered find themselves faced with huge medical bills of which their insurance policies cover only a fraction. Because of the urgency of this tragedy, it is believed that the 1990s will be a decade that experiences an overhaul of our health care system. While several possible solutions have been suggested, two basic plans have emerged as serious contenders in the health care arena. One plan would adopt a single, nationalized health insurance provider; the other opts for a private sector solution that would keep private health insurance companies in place but somehow improve the coverage options for those who now cannot afford health care.

The nationalized health insurance, or single-payer solution, as it is sometimes called, would create a tax-supported health insurance system. All medical costs—for doctor's visits, hopitalization, medication, etc—would be paid for by a single insurer, that is, the federal government. Such a solution would cut overall health care costs by eliminating the amount of paperwork that is currently generated by the present system in which thousands of different types of policies are written by more than 400 separate health insurers, all with their own administrative, overhead and marketing costs. Some suggest that a single-payer system would cut down on the amount of paperwork doctors are faced with as well, since in the present system doctors must either spend an incredible amount of time filling out paperwork in order to be paid by insurance companies or hire a full-time person to take care of this paperwork for them. Another reason given in support of the single-payer system is that in the idealized version of this system, the same quality health care would be given to all in need, regardless of their ability to pay. In the present system, hospitals are known to ration health care based on the patient's ability or insurer's desire to pay. Some opponents to the single-payer system, however, fear that in order to afford to pay for health care for all, the overall quality of health care would suffer.

The private sector solution suggests that private health insurance companies are currently serving many people very well, and should thus continue to do so. However, it is an undeniable fact that tens of millions of people are not being served by the existing private health insurance system or by the present welfare system designed to care for those who cannot afford private health care. Several options have been offered as a way to keep the private sector insurance system in place while implementing a system to cover those presently not covered. One private sector solution would simply expand and improve the existing welfare mechanisms—Medicaid for the poor, and Medicare for those over 65—to supply coverage for all now not covered under the private sector. Another solution would rely on the existing private insurance companies to improve the present situation. In this plan the government would offer them business and tax incentives to expand and improve their coverage to include all who are not not currently insured; such a plan would, thus, expect the problem to be solved with a minimum of governmental control.

A solution to this national crisis will most likely not be agreed upon in the immediate future. However, there are some points on which those in favor of either the single payer or the private sector solution would probably find themselves in agreement. First, the problem before them is very complex and no solution will be a simple one. Second, whatever solution is adopted will end up costing a large sum of money, whether it comes directly from the taxpayers themselves or indirectly through business and tax incentives for insurance companies and other businesses. Finally, the fact that a nation as wealthy as the United States has such a large number of people unable to have access to health care is an appalling and tragic situation, and a solution must be found.

QUESTIONS

1. Briefly summarize the single–payer solution to the health care crisis.

_____

_____

2. Briefly summarize the private sector solution to the health care crisis.

_____

_____

3. Which of these two proposed solutions do you think would be better? Why?

_____

_____

TAKING SIDES

Below are statements made by fictitious people in response to the health care crisis and the two solutions proposed in the reading. In small groups read the statements and discuss whether you think the person making the statement would favor the single payer solution or the private sector solution and why you think so.

1. **Dr. Juarez:** I am in my office from 9:00 a.m. until 6:00 p.m. seeing patients. And then after all the patients have left, I have two to three more hours to spend filling out insurance forms. It seems like every patient has a different kind of form. It takes ten minutes just to figure out what information goes where on which form. If I don't keep up on the paperwork, I won't get paid. Since I have a small private practice, I don't want to hire a person to just fill out insurance forms, because I would then have to charge my patients more.

_____

_____

2. **Susan Fromer:** Last year when I went in for my yearly check-up, my doctor noticed a black mole on my arm that I had never thought twice about. He sent me immediately to a specialist for a biopsy. The biopsy

showed some cancerous tissue, but since I got immediate treatment the problem was solved. I'm so thankful that I have the best medical care possible. I don't mind paying more as long as I know I'm paying for quality, because when it comes to your health, cost is no objective.

_____

_____

3. **John Chen:** Once a month I spend a whole day at my grandfather's helping him with his bills. I can't believe how complicated it is. Sure he's got health problems. He's 86 years old. But the health problems are nothing compared to the mess he's faced with in paying the bills. Trying to figure out what Medicare has paid and what it still owes is impossible, and I'm an accountant. I can't imagine what would happen if the government were to step in and take over for everyone. The amount of red tape would be disastrous.

_____

_____

4. **Veronica Sims:** Last year I was employed full time and had health insurance through my company. I started getting sick a lot, and eventually the doctor told me I was HIV–positive. She started me on treatments right away. I've been able to keep my job, but my insurance company dropped me because they say the treatments are too expensive. I don't know how I'm going to be able to afford them now.

_____

_____

5. **Dave Smith:** I haven't been sick a day in my life, knock on wood. But I know I've got good health insurance if I ever need it. I have a friend at work who ended up in the hospital for a week. When he got the bill, he couldn't believe it! But luckily, his insurance paid for almost the whole amount. I know there are lots of people who aren't as lucky as I or my friend, and I agree that something has to be done. But the system works

for a lot of us. Why throw something out that isn't broken?

_____

_____

FINAL TEAM TASK: ROUND TABLE DISCUSSION

A round table discussion is like a debate except that there are no teams involved. Instead, it involves a discussion among individuals who have some specific knowledge about a given topic. The question to be discussed at your round table discussion is: **What should be done about the current health care crisis?**

1. Each member of the discussion should take one of the following roles:
    a. Mr. George Jones, CEO of Executive Health Insurance Company
    b. Prof. Amanda Morris, chairperson of the Public Health Department at Harris University
    c. Dr. Eric Honda, head of an AIDS clinic in a large metropolitan area
    d. Dr. Sharon Glass, a famous plastic surgeon
    e. Congressman Stan Drew, a congressman up for reelection in a wealthy, mostly suburban district
    f. The Moderator, who starts and moderates the discussion
2. Before your discussion begins, consider what each of the designated individuals may think about the issue.
3. The discussion begins with the Moderator, who introduces all of the members to each other and states the question to be discussed. The discussion proceeds with the members speaking up when they feel they have a point to make. The moderator should try to keep any one speaker from dominating the discussion and make sure that all members contribute.
4. The discussion ends with the Moderator giving a short summary of the discussion.

FINAL WRITTEN TASK

Write a one– to two–page essay that gives an overview of the health care system in your country. Include in this essay a general description of how the system is designed to work and a discussion of a problem within the system.

Segment 12

The Perfect Baby: A Follow-Up

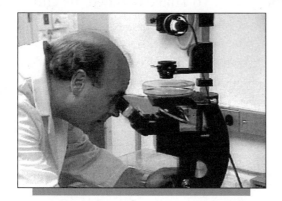

from *Nightline*, 7/18/90
Runtime: 8:09
Begin: 01:51:35

Previewing

KEY QUESTIONS

1. What is the state of genetic engineering today?
2. What advances are expected in the near future?
3. How will these advances change our lives and the lives of future generations?
4. Should legal action be taken to guard against some possible effects of genetic engineering?

DISCUSSION

1. If you could find out whether you or your spouse had a good possibility of contributing the gene for a serious disease to your future children, would you take a test to determine this information?

   _____

   _____

2. If it were possible to choose the physical characteristics of your baby, such as eye color, hair color, and height, would you do so? Why or why not?

   _____

   _____

PREDICTION

In small groups, brainstorm about the possible consequences of scientific advances that would allow a parent to discover facts about his or her future children. What are some positive and negative consequences that could result from such advances? Write down three consequences under each heading below. Confirm your predictions after you have watched the entire segment once.

POSITIVE CONSEQUENCES	NEGATIVE CONSEQUENCES
1. _____	_____
2. _____	_____
3. _____	_____

ESSENTIAL WORDS TO KNOW

The *italicized* items in the following sentences are used in this video segment. After reading the sentences, match each term with its definition from the list.

a. a movement devoted to improving the human race through genetic manipulation

b. the scientific manipulation of genes

c. an imperfection in the makeup of the genes that causes a physical problem

d. examining a person's genes in order to decide whether to keep or discard them

e. someone who assesses risks or rates the acceptability of risks for an insurance policy

_____ 1. Certain *genetic defects* can be discovered before a baby is born.

_____ 2. Scientists are trying to eliminate some birth defects and illnesses through *genetic engineering.*

_____ 3. When the process of *genetic screening* becomes more advanced, it may be possible to predict the future occurrence of some genetic diseases.

_____ 4. An *underwriter* determines important aspects of health and life insurance policies.

_____ 5. A number of years ago people involved in the *eugenics* movement wanted to better society by determining human qualities through genetics.

Global Viewing

GETTING THE GENERAL IDEA

The following experts were interviewed about their vision of the consequences of genetic engineering. Watch the entire segment and check whether each expert thinks genetic engineering will have positive or negative consequences.

	POSITIVE CONSEQUENCES	NEGATIVE CONSEQUENCES
1. Dr. James Watson	_____	_____
2. Rep. David Obey	_____	_____
3. Jeremy Rifkin	_____	_____
4. Daniel Kevles	_____	_____
5. Robert Wright	_____	_____

Intensive Viewing

LISTENING CLOZE

Watch this part of the segment and fill in the blanks with the missing words. Then compare your answers with those of another student

Barbara Walters: Consider this scenario. A brutal _____

orders a team of _____ scientists to create blond, blue-eyed, strong, brilliant men and women, the perfect people, a _____ _____. In creating this, he tries to find out what genes cause disease, mental illness, physical _____ , indeed, people he just doesn't like. All of this by mapping out the _____ blueprint. _____ _____? Well, those of us who remember World War II and Adolf Hitler aren't so sure.

Now consider this. What if a prospective employer or an insurance company could look at a _____ of your _____? And because of a propensity toward a certain disease, determine that you are "undesirable" or, at the very least, _____. As Steve Shepard tells us, the issues we've raised are not as _____ or as far off as you may think.

GETTING THE IMPORTANT INFORMATION

Read the questions below. Then as you watch the rest of the segment, circle the best answer to each question.

1. Why did James Watson and Francis Crick win the Nobel Prize?
   a. They started a scientific revolution.
   b. They counted the number of genes.
   c. They discovered the structure of DNA.
   d. All of the above.

2. What is so important about DNA?
   a. It contains approximately 100,000 genes.
   b. It can cure genetic disorders before children are conceived.
   c. It contains human tissue that causes disease.
   d. All of the above.

3. What information can be found out from a person's genes?
   a. certain physical characteristics
   b. the possibility that a couple's future child may have a genetic disorder
   c. the possibility that an adult may develop a specific disease
   d. all of the above

4. What is the goal of the Human Genome Project?
   a. to map the entire human genetic system
   b. to predetermine a person's physical and mental characteristics
   c. to create a master race
   d. to eliminate all disease

5. What does Dr. Watson believe the results of the Human Genome Project will do?
   a. help scientists discover the meaning of life
   b. help scientists understand the genetic aspect of many diseases
   c. help scientists understand the molecular aspect of cancer
   d. both a and b

6. What are Rep. Obey's fears about genetic engineering?
   a. Genetic information will be used by employers in choosing employees.
   b. Genetic information will be used by insurance companies to discover what diseases a person may develop in the future.
   c. Genetic information will cause employers to screen employees for drugs.
   d. Both a and b.

7. What are Daniel Kevles' fears about genetic engineering?
   a. Ethical considerations are not being considered in genetic research.
   b. Parents will want to create perfect babies.
   c. People will try to control the composition of the gene pool by social policy.
   d. None of the above.

8. What does Robert Wright fear?
   a. New genetic diseases could be created.
   b. Insurance companies will use genetic information in writing insurance policies.
   c. Some parents won't be able to afford the high cost of curing genetic diseases.
   d. A new form of social stratification may result after several generations.

Language Focus

UNDERSTANDING IDIOMS

Guess the meaning of the *italicized* idiom in each sentence. Then choose the statement that has the meaning most similar to the original sentence.

1. Many of our illnesses are due to bad genes, which is simply bad luck. Those who believe genetic engineering can make life better don't believe a person should be condemned to suffer because of the *throw of the dice*.*
   a. Those who believe genetic engineering can make life better don't believe a person should suffer because of chance.
   b. Those who believe genetic engineering can make life better don't believe a person should suffer because he likes to gamble.
   c. Those who believe genetic engineering can make life better don't believe a person should suffer because he wants to.

2. Rep. Obey worries that employers may try to *rule people out* of a job if they don't have a good genetic makeup.
   a. Rep. Obey worries that employers may try to make rules against people who don't have a good genetic makeup.
   b. Rep. Obey worries that employers may try to fire people who have genetic illnesses.
   c. Rep. Obey worries that employers may try exclude people from a job if they don't have a good genetic makeup.

*A common variation of this idiom is *a toss of the dice*.

137

3. Some people may want to manipulate the composition of the human gene pool; they will try to *root out* and destroy bad genes and encourage the proliferation of good ones.
   ⓐ Some people may want to manipulate the composition of the human gene pool; they will try to find and destroy the bad genes and encourage the proliferation of good ones.
   b. Some people may want to manipulate the composition of the human gene pool; they will try to grow and destroy the bad genes and encourage the proliferation of good ones.
   c. Some people may want to manipulate the composition of the human gene pool; they will try to freeze and destroy the bad genes and encourage the proliferation of good ones.

4. Americans get *riled up* about the superiority of foreign products; imagine how they would feel about another nation creating a superior race.
   a. Americans get confused and sad about the superiority of foreign products; imagine how they would feel about another nation creating a superior race.
   b. Americans get tired of hearing about the superiority of foreign products; imagine how they would feel about another nation creating a superior race.
   ⓒ Americans get angry and agitated about the superiority of foreign products; imagine how they would feel about another nation creating a superior race.

LISTENING FOR FIGURATIVE LANGUAGE

At times speakers in the video segment used figurative, rather than literal, language to make you think about the true meaning of their words. Listen to the following excerpts and fill in the blanks with the figurative phrase.

01:55:55- **Dr. Watson:** Cancer is a disease we are getting nowhere with in
01:55:50
understanding at the molecular level. And now we're moving in it very fast, so I think in 25 years we'll know most of the important facts.

01:56:45- **Steve Shepard:** So far, so good. Knowledge benefiting mankind. But, (a)
01:56:59
_____ _____ , _____ _____ _____ _____
_____ , genetic research, and the genetic screening of individuals also have a potential downside.

Steve Shepard: Many who follow developments in genetic research think laws must be passed to protect individuals from abuse.

Rep. Obey: Right now, I think the ethical considerations are _____ (b)
_____ ____ _____ _____ when they ought to be in
tandem with the _____ _____ _____ _____
on the research.

Now suggest the meaning of each phrase as it relates to the context.

(a) _____

(b) _____

CONSIDERING FUTURE SITUATIONS

In the video people expressed thoughts about the future consequences of
genetic engineering. Some things they felt certain about; others they felt
had only the possibility of happening. The modal (*might, will, could,* etc.)
used in their statements showed how certain they felt that an event would
occur. Read the following statements. How certain are the speakers about
the consequences they mention? Check the appropriate column and
underline the modal for each statement below.

	CERTAIN	LESS CERTAIN
1. In 25 years we'll know most of the important facts about cancer.	_____	_____
2. Someday employers will screen applicants for their genetic makeup.	_____	_____
3. Insurance companies say they won't get into genetics.	_____	_____
4. Parents might take advantage of the technology.	_____	_____
5. Some parents will want to determine their future children's physical and mental characteristics.	_____	_____
6. This could produce a new form of social stratification.	_____	_____
7. There could be poor average children on the one hand and rich superchildren on the other.	_____	_____
8. Some people may want to control the composition of the gene pool by social policy.	_____	_____

Now work in pairs to come up with at least three more consequences that you think *will*, *might*, or *could* happen when genetic engineers can map the human genetic system. Write them below.

1. _____

2. _____

3. _____

Postviewing

COMPARING CULTURES

Discuss the following questions in small groups.

1. Were you surprised or shocked by anything you learned in this video?

2. Knowledge about genetics is already used in the United States to determine whether the embryos pregnant women over the age of 35 are carrying have certain genetic diseases. Do you think this kind of genetic testing is good or not? Explain your answer.

3. The U.S. government has been very supportive of the Human Genome Project. Do you think this is a good project to support? Why or why not?

4. Problems concerning ethics and the advancement of scientific and medical issues like those discussed in the video have become so important that a relatively new field has developed in U.S. universities called Biomedical Ethics. What are some issues that you can imagine are discussed in such a field?

5. Are you aware of projects similar to the Human Genome Project in your own country? If so, what are some of the problems they investigate?

6. Are people in your country worried about issues related to genetic engineering? If so, what specifically are some of their worries?

Read the article *Making a Better Baby* and answer the comprehension and opinion questions that follow.

Making a Better Baby

If you want to buy a dog, you consider the characteristics that are important to you. A dog to accompany you through the woods on hunting trips? Maybe a retriever or setter appeals to you. A vicious guard dog to watch over your house while you're away? Perhaps you'll want a Doberman or possibly a pit bull. You know that certain breeds have specific strengths, because people have been crossbreeding animals for centuries in order to improve the desired qualities in a given breed. But when a couple decides to have a baby, beyond jokingly hoping that maybe it won't inherit get it's father's nose or it's grandmother's bad teeth, a healthy infant is all that is really wished for.

However, the Repository for Germinal Choice in Escondido, California, gives a woman the chance to set her hopes much higher than simply a healthy child. The Repository for Germinal Choice was founded in 1981 by Robert Graham and has facilitated the births of 156 babies as of April 1992. In the beginning Graham's goal was to produce "better babies" by collecting sperm from Nobel Prize winners, which would then be selected by qualified women. The women would be impregnated through artificial insemination with the sperm of their choice, and the result would hopefully be a baby; but not just any baby. This supposedly genetically superior stock would create an improved human being—more intelligent, more creative, maybe even a future leader of men.

Graham's goal has never been realized exactly as he had originally planned. He first encountered difficulties getting Nobel laureates to comply; only three actually donated sperm to the Repository. This Nobel-quality sperm was never chosen by any women, and today is no longer in storage. Graham has since collected samples from a wide range of highly qualified men, including an Olympic gold medalist. While the identity of the sperm donors is confidential, women can choose from detailed descriptions informing them of physical characteristics like height, weight, eye and hair color; ethnic background; professional and other accomplishments; hobbies and interests.

Among the Repository's success stories is Doron Blake, who today at nine years of age charges $500 for an interview. Doron got a computer at the age of two, and is now almost ready to write computer programs. At six his interests included reading and discussing Shakespeare. He has also read the original version, in verse, of Homer's *Illiad* .

No governmental regulations put the legality of an operation like the Repository for Germinal Choice in question. But some experts in the field of medical ethics feel that the ethics of such an operation are questionable. Professor Arthur Caplan, the director of the University of Minnesota's Center for Biomedical Ethics, believes the Repository for Germinal Choice is a dangerous step in the direction of genetic manipulation. Interviewed on *Nightline* ("The

Perfect Baby: A Follow-Up," July 18, 1990), he said that parents should not have a child with the expectation that they can make sure that child will become what they want because they have given him or her the genetic traits to reach their goal. He also said of the Repository for Germinal Choice, "It's eugenic in purpose. I think it should be closed."

COMPREHENSION QUESTIONS

1. What was Graham's original goal in starting the Repository for Germinal Choice?

2. Why wasn't this goal accomplished?

3. What does the Repository for Germinal Choice do?

4. On what basis do women choose the sperm with which they will be impregnated?

5. What doesn't Professor Caplan like about the Repository for Germinal Choice?

6. What does he mean when he says the purpose of the Repository for Germinal Choice is "eugenic"?

IN YOUR OPINION

1. Do you think places like the Repository for Germinal Choice should be allowed to operate? Explain your answer.

_____

_____

2. The identities of the donors is kept confidential at the Repository for Germinal Choice. If a child born with the help of a donor from the Repository for Germinal Choice decides he or she wants to find out who the sperm donor was, do you think he or she has the right to find out this information? Why or why not?

_____

_____

FINAL TEAM TASK

OPTION A: JOBS FOR GENETIC ENGINEERS

Suppose you are a group of genetic engineers creating your own small company. Because the field of genetic engineering is still quite new, you have a wide open market in front of you. Also because of the newness of the field, the general public does not have any idea how genetic engineering could be a service they need. Your task is to tap into the market in as many ways as possible by making your skills applicable to a diverse range of areas.

1. Come up with at least four markets to sell yourselves to: for example, the medical field, insurance companies, fertility clinics, human resource departments (which hire and fire employees for large companies).
2. Devise a detailed plan to educate each market about how it can benefit from genetic engineering and convince it that you have skills they need.
3. Present your plan to the rest of the class, with each member of your group presenting the plan for one market.
4. The members of the class should ask you questions about your plan and then decide which of the plans convinced them to use your services.

OPTION B: MINI-RESEARCH TASK

Scientific advances that affect our lives today are happening far more rapidly than ethical considerations can keep up with. Genetic engineering is one area where ethics and medical advances have clashed, as you have seen and read. Fertility science, the science that develops new methods for helping women to have children, is another area where advances are being made so rapidly that ethical questions have often been raised. Choose one of these two areas — genetic engineering or fertility science — for a mini-research project.

1. Read about the topic you have chosen in books, magazines, or newspapers.
2. Take notes on what you read.
3. Use your notes to give an oral report to the class. Include in your report:
   a. a summary of the information in the articles you read.
   b. three discussion questions for the class — these should NOT be comprehension questions that ask for a factual response, but subjective questions that stimulate a class discussion.

FINAL WRITTEN TASK

OPTION A: WRITING UP YOUR MARKETING PLAN

Write up the marketing plan you developed for the Jobs for Genetic Engineers task. In your written plan, explain why your skills are needed in the market you chose. Be as specific as you can in a plan of approximately one–page long.

OPTION B: SUMMARIZING AND REACTING

Write a one– to two–page essay in which you summarize and react to the ideas presented in the articles you read in the Mini-Research Task. The first part of your essay should be a summary of the notes that you collected during your research. (You may want to check back to the segment "Cheating in College" for information on how to paraphrase when you express other people's thoughts in your essay.) The second part of your essay should be your reaction to some of the ideas you found the most remarkable, either because you were very positively impressed by them or because they had a strong negative impact on you.